a *Play-Full* Life

SLOWING DOWN & SEEKING PEACE

a *Play-Full* Life

SLOWING DOWN & SEEKING PEACE

Jaco J. Hamman

THE
PILGRIM
PRESS
Cleveland

For:
All who once knew how to play.
Michelle
For living a play-full life with me.
Vir die speelruimtes wat jy my bied.
Jami and Michaela
In gratitude for your ability to restore my tickle.
Dankie dat julle altyd my kielie vir my teruggee as ek dit verloor.

The Pilgrim Press
700 Prospect Avenue
Cleveland, Ohio 44115–1100
thepilgrimpress.com

16 15 14 13   5 4 3 2

Library of Congress Cataloging-in-Publication Data
Hamman, Jaco J.
    A play-full life : slowing down and seeking peace / Jaco J. Hamman.
        p.   cm.
    ISBN 978-0-8298-1820-8 (alk. paper)
        1. Play – Religious aspects – Christianity.   I. Title.
    BT709.H36 2011
    233′.5 – dc22   2010049710

Contents

Acknowledgments

In gratitude

All my life I've been exposed to play-full persons whose lives touched me deeply. For a grandmother who knew how to laugh, a mom who knows hospitality, a dad who is a traveler, and more people than I can name: thank you.

Twenty persons covering diverse walks of life and spanning fifty years of life experience commented on drafts of each chapter. To all of you, thank you.

To Kim Martin Sadler and The Pilgrim Press, especially for the grace of extending deadlines, thank you.

I owe a special word of gratitude to Ulrike Guthrie, who edited this book. Uli, this project, our third together, was a pleasure. Your professionalism and ability to awaken the best in your authors are gifts I received. Thank you.

I am indebted to my life partner, Michelle, and daughters, Jami and Michaela. For love, belonging, encouragement, support, time, space, and so much more, thank you.

A final word of gratitude to God, the ultimate Player who played with earth, played with death, and now plays in and through us. Thank God.

a *Play-Full* Life

Introduction

I smelled God. Maybe you have, too. It happened in northern Montana as I was making my way along forest and fire roads on my off-road motorcycle with my riding partner, Barry. We were nearly two thousand miles into our journey already, having left Michigan a few days earlier, but only on Day One of "our ride," and not knowing what the next twenty-five hundred miles would bring as we set our sights on the Mexican border crossing of Antelope Wells, New Mexico. We were on the Continental Divide Trail that follows the Rocky Mountains from Canada all the way south into Mexico. Somewhere I missed a turn and we were lost — again. It had not taken us long to realize that getting lost was going to be an integral experience of this journey.

Asking for directions can be freeing, and soon we were heading back into the Rockies under deep purple clouds. We stopped to don our rain gear just as a torrential storm exploded above and around us. Even with our off-road motorcycles, traveling on gravel in these circumstances is dangerous, so we stopped and took shelter beneath some trees, reckoning on there being taller trees in the area for lightning to strike. A herd of deer nervously crossed the road a few yards from us, sniffing the air as if they knew something we didn't.

The storm blew over in about fifteen minutes, and blue sky appeared. It was then that I smelled God. It was an intense smell that filled not only my nose and lungs but also every fiber of my being. I hadn't known: *God smells like a pine forest freshly washed by a torrential thunderstorm.*

Not worrying excessively when one gets lost and smelling God are both normal experiences if one lives a play-full life. How spiritual and life-giving it is to discover life and nature and God beyond any knowledge or past experience one might have! Smell is a powerful sense that awakens one's spirit and creates new memories just as one can feel particularly alive in a moment of significant adversity.

A few days later, high up in the Rockies and crossing Blow Out Pass in southern Colorado, we found ourselves right below the tree line after riding a ridge of alpine tundra, lost on an impassable trail, and in search of a new way off the mountain. A steep, four-and-a-half mile descent down a washed-out, rock-filled, deeply-rutted two-track awaited us.

With all the concentration I can muster, I'm leading us down the mountain, adrenaline rushing through my veins. After going a few minutes I stop and Barry catches up with me. The terrain is too uneven to dismount, so we just sit a while on our motorcycles catching our breath. Barry interrupts: "Jaco, there's oil running down your drive shaft." Unable to dismount safely, I look over my shoulder and see hydraulic oil flowing from the rear brake-line that has pulled out of its housing. I no longer have a rear brake on my trusty steed, which has previously taken me safely to places such as the Arctic Ocean in northern Alaska and along historic Route 66. We discuss various options, including Barry leaving me to seek help, but it's obvious that no truck would be able to navigate this road. The option of leaving my motorcycle on the mountain and walking out feels like giving in to despair and hopelessness. So I ride my motorcycle down the mountain, using the friction of my clutch and first gear to keep me from a wild and no doubt deadly run down Blow Out Pass. This time the smell of a clutch slowly burning itself up is the only smell I am aware of. I prefer to smell God. I hear nothing but the crunch of rocks and gravel under my tires and the engine working hard to slow my pace, yet I know I have to maintain a speed fast enough to remain upright. Still, I am feeling alive as my mind discerns the best route to take. Every muscle in my body anticipates the movement of my motorcycle as I run over rocks, through deep ruts, and along a precarious drop-off. I am focused, in a definite zone, not feeling anxious or worried but content and hopeful, recognizing this as an unexpected adventure.

When I finally reach the last stage in the descent from Blow Out Pass — the name now forever etched in my mind — smoke is pouring from the engine right under the gas tank. I dismount, thinking that my motorcycle is about to burst into flames, and I remove my tank bag stuffed with valuables. I take the water we carry with us and pour it over the engine to cool the machine. Thankfully no flames appear and the smoke diminishes as the engine cools. Discerning our options, we crunch Granny Smith apples, the tart taste a welcome antidote to the smell of my burnt-out clutch.

Recognizing that the motorcycle is fine other than the broken rear brake and burnt-out clutch, I limp to Albuquerque, more than two hundred miles away. Entering Albuquerque in rush hour and 103 degree heat, I nearly make it to the motorcycle repair shop. A mere third of a mile from help, I opt to call the service truck to come to my rescue. As I am leaving a voicemail for the service manager to ask him to come and pick me up, a man stops at the other side of the intersection and asks me if I need help. Above the noise of the traffic I tell him of my dilemma. Turns out he has a trailer close by and he takes me to the repair shop. This Samaritan, Jared, isn't bothered by my muddy boots, by the fact that I am covered in dust from head to toe, or that I am in desperate need of a shower after a few nights camping. He takes me to the dealership where he hears what repairs my motorcycle needs, offers me the use of a motor vehicle for as long as I need it, and disappears. He knows only my first name. He reappears half an hour later, hands me the keys to a vehicle, and invites us for a steak dinner at his house, where we meet his family.

A play-full person finds liminal, sacred moments, as well as peace, contentment, and hope in the strangest of places and circumstances. Such a one is responsive to the adversities one encounters on the road of life and is open to the generosity and hospitality of Samaritans like Jared. Play-fullness is a way of *being*, which seems contradictory in a world that tells us we will find meaning and purpose in *doing* something. It empowers us to be travelers rather than tourists in life. Play-fullness opens us to experience God and others anew; it empowers us to be responsive to the twists and turns in life rather than going down the road of anxious reactivity; it allows us to be guests to someone else's hospitality.

No doubt you have noticed I talk about being play-full and about play-fullness rather than about *play*. Play is important to our lives and much is being written about play. Unfortunately, the term "play" has been co-opted by other industries, such as the gambling industry, in which one "plays the slots," and the sex industry, which offers us "playmates." We "play" on the stock market. Here, play has become a consumer good. *Play is most often seen as a purposeless, unproductive, even useless, yet restorative activity, an escape of sorts reserved for special moments such as weekends and vacations.* More and more, play costs money. Yet play comes naturally to us in childhood. Through it we improve capacities, such as problem-solving skills, and meet specific needs, such as letting go, needing to take risks, exerting control or being controlled, feeling empowered, and being connected. Furthermore, play helps us discover the importance both of setting boundaries and engaging others and instills in us a love for culture and art. It helps us manage our destructiveness and rejuvenates the mind, much like deep sleep does. Play improves our health. Stress is toxic to our bodies, but play helps to strengthen our immune system, fighting off illnesses and opportunistic diseases leading to fewer symptoms such as food or environmental allergies, migraine headaches, asthma, gastrointestinal illnesses, and more.

Play-fullness draws on these gifts that play offers us without buying into the dichotomous thinking that pits playing against working or that sees playing as wasting time. Furthermore, play-fullness can never be confused with life-depriving activities such as gambling and those offered by the sex industry. Play-fullness cannot be bought, for it is determined by the quality of our relationships.

To be play-full is to imaginatively and creatively engage one's self, others, God, and all of reality so that peace and justice reign within us and with others, and in every conceivable situation we might find ourselves in. We are players who received the promise of "life to the full" from Jesus. Peace and justice speaks to restored relationships and meaning that defines health. It anticipates hearing and seeing afresh, and it empowers in a way that offers freedom to you and to others. Furthermore, peace and justice lead us to touch and be touched by those persons marginalized in our world and to work toward changing structures that oppress. A life of peace and justice is good news to us and to others. Yet play-fullness is not limited to something we do; it is not the opposite of "working" or "doing" or "loving." Rather, it informs leisure and labor, the sacred and the profane. To be play-full is not to be irrelevant or irreverent, nor does it remove us from reality. With my motorcycle becoming less and less roadworthy and with our having to descend a precarious mountain without maps, our situation was serious. Yet we could be play-full because we did not let worry and fear consume us. Being play-full encourages us to be mindful about our reality and to engage it with all our heart, mind, and soul — with our whole being. Serious persons, of course, might think that being play-full is frivolous, even a sign of immaturity, forgetting that play-fullness is a sign that God's shalom, God's reign of peace and justice, has set in.

There are many play-full persons who live "life to the full" even in adversity. Anna, for example, remained play-full even in the final moments of her life. I met her as a hospital chaplain when she was dying of cancer. The nurses were concerned about her; they felt she was in denial about the severity of her illness and the fact that her death was imminent. When I entered the room, however, I sensed peace and hope. Anna was not in denial, but with poetic precision shared how her body tells her that her days are few. "My breaths are getting shallower and shallower," she told me in a soft voice. She said she was afraid of the unknown, but the way in which she said that was not a confession. And she added that what lies ahead for her would remove any fear she now has. With creative imagination she envisioned her last moments in this life and what heaven would look like. Anna was play-full with images from memory and Scripture and tradition, experiencing a deep sense of calm and that things would be "OK," even in her death. Her favorite line was: "I ask God often to grant me the privilege to be alive when I die." Anna lived a play-full life, even as she was dying. Hers was a spaciousness that could hold her fear and anticipation of dying and not be overwhelmed by death.

Cultivating "Spaciousness"

Play-fullness, first and foremost, speaks to our inwardness. The core of our being determines how we live life. There is *spaciousness* to being play-full, for potential and possibility enter into the space created *within* us and *between* us and others. The spaciousness within us allows us to feel loving and vital, at peace, flexible, and even hospitable and compassionate. Likewise, space is created *between* us and others as we become God's love and peace to others or as we are pulled into an experience. Imagine for a moment such peace and justice defining your intimate relationships. What would be different for you and about you?

The qualities that play-fullness awakens in us create life-giving relationships with others. It never comes at the cost of others. Think about the space created *between* you and a poem, a book, a novel, or a movie as you are "pulled into" the experience. Yet we also find space *outside* our beings as we recognize a world much bigger than our own needs and desires. As spiritual persons, we are invited to partake in something bigger than what our own creativity produces. Christians call that something bigger God's reign or kingdom. *Within, between, and without*: the directions and places where we live require a sense of spaciousness, boundlessness, roominess. It's no surprise that Jesus said that in heaven there is a house with many rooms. He is the Alpha and the Omega and the vast distance between the beginning and the end. Jesus' own spaciousness toward children, women, the sick and lame, even tax collectors and sinners, portrayed a bigger reality — the roominess of God.

Find a way to reflect the spaciousness of God to someone else.

On a solo motorcycle ride to the Colorado Rockies a few years ago, I decided to travel through South Dakota and Wyoming to see a herd of bison. Born and raised in Africa, I have experienced large herds of Cape buffalo and other wild animals roaming areas so vast they never encounter a fence. As I came over a rolling hill in Wyoming, my motorcycle alarmed a herd of bison. My excitement at seeing bison became exhilaration as the whole herd started to run. Above the engine noise and vibration of my motorcycle, and through a full-face helmet with earplugs, I heard and felt the thunder of hundreds of hooves pounding the earth. I slowed down to about twenty-five miles an hour and the herd and I became one. We ran parallel to each other for a quarter mile or so and suddenly they stopped. Some lay down and others began to graze again, snorting for air. I was in awe.

The roominess of play-fullness allows our emotions, thoughts, and experiences to roam, even run. But unlike the metaphorical bull in a china shop, a spacious self experiences much without becoming a danger to self or others. Just as the vast plain held the startled bison herd, so too our spaciousness holds not only our emotions and experiences, but also the lives of our loved ones, friends, and even strangers. There is also room for Mother Nature. No longer are our emotions or thoughts at risk of breaking through or spilling over. As a spacious person, for example, you allow yourself to be sad, without fear of "going to pieces" or "losing it." Sadness that roams rarely becomes depression and rarely leads to isolation or alienation. A spacious person's anger rarely becomes volcanic-like violence that wounds others, for that person is able to be hospitable to self and others.

A play-full person seldom feels confined by the dichotomies of life, such as being rational or irrational, ill or healthy, or by the inevitable realities of time, place, money, community, and limited abilities and opportunity. Within every limitation, every boundary or rule, a spacious person still finds ways to be play-full — in fact does so habitually. As Anna showed us, one can be play-full even in the final moments of life, embracing one's own death and anticipating a life beyond the grave.

Balancing "The Four P's of Life"

Today we are in great need of such play-fullness. We work longer hours than any previous generation; we sleep less than our bodies need to rejuvenate themselves; we have more debt and insecurities as we live with new economic and safety threats; we experience job loss in record numbers; and we fear that our national security will be breached. Our health care system is uncertain; consumerism remains high and has become a second birthright as we self-medicate our stress by shopping; our family systems are strained and we are separating and divorcing at record levels; our children face new diagnoses such as Attention Deficit Hyperactivity Disorder (ADHD); organized religion in the United States is rapidly declining; and nature is exploited to levels that cannot sustain the long-term future of humanity. To experience the promise of "life to the full" in these circumstances offers not only hope, but also promises ways to reverse some of these trends.

Such full or abundant life is possible for all, and this book is written for all who identify in some way with the previous paragraph. But it is written also for all those for whom, as Sigmund

Freud said shortly before his death, balancing loving and working is the most important and difficult task of life. As a husband and father, I too find balancing loving and working a challenge. How does one find communion and build community with loved ones and friends if one is also building a career in a seemingly insatiable corporate world? Of course my struggle is not unique, but it certainly is pervasive in Western culture in general and in North American culture specifically.

How do you balance loving and working?

A South African by birth and holding an African worldview, I know that there are different ways of experiencing time and community. Two proverbs beautifully describe the differences between a North American worldview and an African worldview. The African proverb "The people who love me grow on me like moss" refers to the medicinal qualities of moss, meaning that when the blows of life assail us, our friends become a soothing balm that protects and restores. The North American proverb, by contrast, states: "A rolling stone gathers no moss." Many of us are rolling stones, encouraged by false promises to believe that constantly moving on will lead to happiness and wealth. All of us, however, long for the soothing balm of sustaining friendships that can help ease the hurts of life.

Likewise, African hospitality with its keen awareness of the communal ties that bind us all together looks and feels very different from North American hospitality. As a psychotherapist, I listen to many stories of individuals who try to find meaning in life's circumstances. And as a marriage and family therapist, I regularly encounter couples and families yearning for more life-giving ways to be in relationship. I am also an ordained clergyperson and think many faith communities are ineffective in helping people live a play-full life or to be play-full with God.

I wrote this book because I am mindful of the need and importance of balancing personhood, partnering, parenthood, and profession in life.

* *Personhood* speaks to being a healthy self, a healthy "I" or "me." Healthy personhood, which is not defined by the absence of disease but by the presence of meaning, is not a given, but takes much conscious cultivation. Yet such attention to the self is often confused with being "narcissistic" or "egocentric." Play-fullness deepens our relationships, as Anna's relationship with her self deepened even as she awaited death.

* *Partnering* includes all our intimate relationships, from friendships to marriage and family. Our partnerships become the relational web that anchors us in the ups and downs of life. Partnering also includes the partnership we have with the earth, which graciously sustains us. Play-full persons never exploit their life-giving relationships.

* *Parenting*, as you imagine, addresses parenthood, but includes all roles and activities that strengthen children and those not yet adults. It is being a big brother or a big sister, or being an uncle or aunt, and being a grandma or grandpa to someone. Many sociologists believe that the biggest concern the United States faces is not terrorism or global warming, but the quality of the daycare and other nurturing we offer the current young generation as they build stable intrapersonal and interpersonal foundations.

* *Profession* is about our work and sense of vocation. It includes the vocation of being a mother and a father or caregiver. In the corporate world in which we live, profession is often a dominant force that undermines personhood, partnering, and parenting.

These "four P's" describe a sequence of sorts that is important to honor, protect, and nurture. Not tending to these in the proper sequence leads to stress and dysfunction. It takes a healthy person to assure a healthy partnership. Likewise, it takes a healthy parenting partnership to effectively raise children. Whatever degree of health we have in these first three P's, we bring into the fourth — our profession. Sadly, this sequence of life is often reversed in our lives, with our profession coming first and our own personhood last. Burnout and feeling overwhelmed or stretched too far are but a few results of this confused sequence.

In what sequence would you place your "Four P's of life": Personhood, Partnering, Parenting, and Profession?

Balancing "the four P's of life" is best done qualitatively and not quantitatively. By this I mean we do well to measure this balance not so much by the amount of time we spend but by the nature of our relationships. The vast majority of us spend more time engaging our profession compared to engaging in the self-care of our personhood. A play-full person has a balance. Does your partner and do your children not only *know* but also *feel* they are more important to you than your work? Do they find themselves competing with your profession to be recognized and loved, always seeing half of your face while the other half is hidden behind a laptop? Does your child's mind have to jump all over the place, in ADHD-like fashion, to keep up with you or the rhythms of your family? Being aware of what really is happening enables you to begin restoring some sense of balance.

So where do you begin? Recognizing the sequence of personhood, partnering, parenting, and profession is a definite first step. *But where is God?* you may ask. *Should God not be the first in this sequence?* Even though it feels religious and possibly pious or even spiritual to say that we have to put God first in our lives, the statement is meaningless unless we *embody* our relationship with God in a personal way. We cannot honor God in any other way than through "the four P's of life." Thus, God needs not so much to be first in some sequence as to be an intimate part of every aspect of our lives: God invites you personally into a relationship that you need to nurture and cultivate (Personhood); as the essence of relationality, God wants to be part of your intimate relationships (Partnering); since God is the Covenant God of future generations, God cares about children and their plight (Parenting); and, God provides you with a sense of vocation and purpose (Profession).

Most persons and families find balancing "the four P's of life" difficult. I certainly do! As with most balancing acts, the important thing is not to keep balance all the time, but to recognize when we have lost that balance — something that happens many times a day — and to restore that balance as soon as possible. Despite the frightening visual image of seeing someone toppling off a high wire or balance beam and the person getting hurt, losing balance in life does not tend to hurt our relationships or us per se. The real danger for us is losing balance and then *remaining in that off-balance position.* Becoming play-full is arguably one of the most effective ways to restore lost balance in our lives. How do we do that?

This weekend, redefine "Thank God it's Friday" by doing something that will nurture your soul.

We nurture play-fullness to feel and be different, and to do so as selves that engage others and God. We desire peace; we long to love in strong relationships; we wish to creatively engage the world and reach our potential; we hope to feel less anxious, less worried, less angry, less burdened, and less fearful. We want to have a different attitude toward life as we reclaim and awaken the image of God in us. In our anxious and uncertain times, a sense of play-fullness offers us new opportunities of engagement as well as a new attitude toward life. Imagine vitality returning to your being as you anticipate the next experience with a sense of hope! Play-fullness as a way of life is rooted, redeemed, and restored, a life that resonates with the desires of God.

Ben, a business consultant, did not receive the promotion he believed he had earned. Initially the sense of rejection was painful, and he defended this with anger and moments of depression. Yet as an essentially play-full person, with time he resumed playing. In particular, he resumed playing with time itself, reminding himself that God, the Creator of time, is also above time. He asked himself what he would tell about this experience to someone today. Then he asked himself what he would tell three months from now. He imagined the conversation three years from now and thirty years from now. As Ben played with time, he recognized that thirty years from now, the pain he feels now may be a mere blip on his life's radar screen. This awareness lessened his sense of rejection significantly, reduced his anger, and lifted his depression. He decided to continue in his current position while keeping options open for new employment.

As a play-full person, you turn moments of conflict into moments of connection, overcoming a natural tendency to withdraw into silence or to lash out in rage. Sarah, in much frustration and growing anger, stared at her defiant four-year-old daughter, Abby, as if she could force her daughter into submission through her gaze. They were in the parking lot of a shopping center and Abby was refusing to climb out of the car. Sarah called upon her play-full self and with a friendly face she started talking with Abby in a mute voice while making exaggerated hand movements and facial expressions. Abby, now caught off-guard by her mom, looked puzzled and the conversation soon changed from one about control to one of asking where Mom's voice is. Every time Abby smiled, Sarah made a sound, initially just a word or two at a time. As Abby started laughing, Sarah resumed talking in a normal voice, asking Abby to get ready to go shopping. Abby thought it was a great idea and asked if they could use the shopping cart with the video screen.

Research shows that activities such as the ones Ben and Sarah engaged in stimulate and develop the brain's frontal cortex, the part of our brain that is responsible for cognition and its processes. It keeps us from slipping into the reactive part of our brains that fuels responses without much thought as to what might be an appropriate response. Those behaviors most often originate in a part of our brains that is called "the reptilian brain." By deliberately turning away from their reactive responses and searching for solutions, Ben could envision a future that does not begin by handing in a resignation letter and Sarah could engage Abby without resorting to anger and conflict.

A Path of Reclamation

You have many childhood memories of being play-full even though you may not be able to recall them at this time, for play-fullness is part of growing up. You engaged yourself in creative, life-giving ways by pretending you were a superhero or a favorite animal or inviting fantasy friends for tea or a meal. All along you were shaped and formed by others, and you allowed fantasy to enrich your life, encouraged by *Mickey, Mr. Rogers, Barney,* and other characters. Sadly, most of us got messages along the way that play-fullness is not appreciated. Or we were play-full and were shamed or wounded by authority figures who had to be serious when we were play-full, leaving us feeling small and insecure but filled with helpless anger and rage.

Children, of course, do not have exclusive claim on play-fullness. Every person, not just the young at heart, can grow into becoming a play-full person. Herb, a retired business executive, assists persons with severe disabilities in swimming pools where they receive aquatic therapy. His witness is that in the interaction between him and these friends, something changes within him, with the result that he receives far more than he gives. Herb, who also took up painting later in life while serving his community through many volunteer opportunities, is a play-full individual living creatively.

To grow into play-fullness is almost always an act of reclamation and restoration, reclaiming a part of our lives that we lost somewhere along the road of life. Play-fullness rehumanizes us. By seeking play-fullness, we are on a path of reclamation, anticipating the image of God manifesting through us. Many times, however, we do not reflect this image in a way that honors God. Ben reclaimed a part of him that induces self-shame as he revisited a painful rejection he had in childhood. Likewise, Sarah empowered herself to feel less helpless and overcame the guilt feelings she carries that she is a bad mother when she yells at Abby in anger.

What part of you that got lost along the way would you like to reclaim by becoming play-full?

Somehow we forget that play-full and creative living touches all worlds in which we live, whether our own inner world or the world around us. Many of us would rather watch others at play than engage in play-full behavior ourselves. We become observers and rarely participants. It is no coincidence that as our own uncertainties and anxieties mount, we are willing to pay large sums of money to watch and admire professional players.

Anticipating a Play-full Life

As I wrote *A Play-full Life*, I envisioned intelligent and curious readers who may not be knowledgable about play-fullness, but who intuit it and already are reclaiming and cultivating such a life in small but significant ways. I imagined all kinds of stressors in the readers' lives that prohibit or diminish a sense of play-fullness, and I wanted to introduce them to many folk I know who have grown in becoming play-full. The chapters that follow can be read as standalone chapters, but chapters 3, 4, 5 may make more sense after reading chapters 1 and 2.

Chapter 1 asks: *What keeps us from being play-full?* The chapter identifies six forces of personhood and culture that place our well-being at risk. The enemies of being and becoming play-full are:

- *Criticism* ("Being play-full is foolishness or childish" or "I have no play-full bone in my body")

- *Control* ("This vacation *will* be fun" or "You will do this!")

- *Compulsion* ("I *have* to do this . . ." or "Doing this makes me less anxious . . .")

- *Competition* ("Winning is everything" or "I hate losing")

- *Conflict* ("I hate myself" or "I hate you")

- *Consumption* ("Give me more" or "I find happiness in buying/security in my debt")

Within these attitudes one finds various forms of individual and communal play that have become corrupted: violence, addictions, pornography, eating disorders, and many more.

Chapters 2 and 3 identify "play-full practices" that foster a sense of play-fullness in us: Realness, Boundlessness, Slowness (chapter 2) and Creativity, Hospitality, and Transcendence (chapter 3). Creative living invites you to use and nurture your imagination. Hospitality calls on you to create space for yourself and others in which you and your guests experience growth. Realness challenges you to hold paradox and resist dichotomous thinking. Boundlessness beckons you to move beyond a life constrained by boundaries and limits, beyond a life that knows only winners and losers. Slowness encourages you to do things at the right speed, to savor the tastes, smells, sights, and sounds of life; to touch life gently and not to "skim" (or move fast) through time and over the earth.

Likewise, transcendence offers you a third area of living between objective reality and your own subjective experience. It is here that you engage in culture and meet God.

Chapter 4 is "Being play-full when alone." In this chapter I apply the play-full practices introduced in the previous chapters to our personal lives. Play-fullness often eludes us when we are alone, for the enemies of play-fullness manifest themselves as we relieve boredom or seek inappropriate ways to self-soothe when alone. Chapter 5 addresses "Being play-full with others." Here I explore visions of play-fullness in intimate relationships. We look at play-fullness in intimate relationships, whether couples, families, or larger groups. Chapter 6 follows the same pattern as the previous two chapters as it addresses "Being play-full with God." Being play-full in your relationship with God, individually and in corporate settings such as churches or in worship, creates the space for you to discover God anew as the "Other." Our relationship with God and corporate worship experiences are both play-full spaces.

The conclusion anticipates that some readers might still ask *How do I become play-full?* The answer to this question of *How?* is *Yes!* One becomes play-full by being rooted, redeemed, and restored, and by engaging in play-full activities, such as imagining one's death, playing with time, expressing oneself in a mute voice, or engaging other play-full practices discussed here.

To be play-full is to imaginatively and creatively engage one's self, others, God, and all of reality so that peace and justice reign within you and with others, and in every conceivable situation in which you might find yourself. This book explores this broad definition of being play-full and as such is a book on what it means to be a human being living with freedom and responsibility before God, with others, and in the world. It is a book that encourages you to reclaim your humanity when forces from without or within have robbed you of the peace that accompanies such freedom. It is also a book on justice and resistance, resisting the ways the world has developed that render persons anxious, fearful, obsessed, hopeless, and violent. Such is their power that these dehumanizing forces touch everyone.

Though a book on resistance, this is not a "how to" book, even if many examples of play-fullness will encourage you to experiment living your life differently and seeing the world anew. It is, however, a book about an embodied life characterized by play-fullness. I hope that *A Play-full Life* will become a conversation partner to you as you grow emotionally, relationally, and spiritually. Such growth is impossible without engaging self, others, God, and the world in new and creative ways. Just as children discover their identity through play behavior and learn how to manage life through playing, you may discover a way of living deeply and passionately between the pages of this book and your own life. Blessings on this journey! You may never be the same again.

ONE

The Enemies of
Becoming Play-full

We are gardens; we are also gardeners. We cultivate play-full selves in others and ourselves. We fertilize with good compost, water, protect against excessive heat and cold and destructive insects, prune deadhead growth that has died, loosen soil, add mulch, and more. And if we do that regularly, we can anticipate a play-full self that grows in us and awakens the play-full selves of others. Showing someone the roominess of God or the spaciousness within us is but one way we cultivate play-full selves. Any experienced gardener engaging this metaphor, no doubt, will remind me that I left out an important and time-consuming component of being a gardener: Weeding!

How simple it would be if we could be play-full without much effort. Yet, as the title of this chapter suggests, there are numerous enemies of play that greatly diminish or even completely prohibit our being play-full. Without your attention and persistent mindfulness, a weed such as *criticism* will enter your life without you even noticing. At a recent soccer match for six-year-old girls, Hailey's dad kept shouting at her to pass the ball to her playmates. "Pass, Pass!" and "Hang back!" and "GO, GO, GO!" and "Think, Think, Think!" crowded the air. One could see how Hailey, stuck between hanging back and going, tried her utmost for her dad. Overwhelmed by confusion, she hung back when she needed to go and passed the ball when she could have kicked for a goal. Criticism is but one enemy of play-fullness, one that comes naturally to all who were raised by parents and teachers who believed that

21

pointing out to children their mistakes is an effective way to cultivate the life of a child. Criticism, however, most often cultivates inferiority or shame.

Along with the other enemies of play-fullness, what makes criticism such a presence in our lives is that it is a *corrupted form of attempts at play-fullness*. Whether it is *criticism, control, compulsion, competition, conflict, or consumption,* these enemies of play-fullness all have a hint of play-fullness in them. Some might even argue that they are forms of play. The fruits of these forces, however, are not peace and justice, but frustration, fear, and inner fragmentation. Furthermore, these forces become part of hurtful behaviors such as addictions, eating disorders, and interpersonal violence.

How do you partner with others to curb
your destructive potential?

As you read this chapter, prepare yourself to look in a mirror. The image of a garden long neglected may be scary or just plain ugly, for the enemies of play expose a side of us we rarely own, the side where our sinfulness, our aggression, and our destructiveness reside. If you befriend your criticism, for example, it will change your life in significant ways. What would happen if Hailey's dad were to tell his six-year-old over breakfast one morning:

Dad can be nasty toward you at times and I do not appreciate that part of myself. When I become nasty and critical of you, I imagine you feel like a snail that wants to crawl back into its shell, for it feels like no matter what you do, you cannot be good enough. Honey, when you feel that I am nasty toward you, will you tell me so that I stop? I'd rather tell you how much I love you and how proud I am of you, especially when you are playing soccer.

If Hailey's dad is play-full with his criticism, his daughter might reach the potential she already shows. As a play-full person you can be play-full even with those parts of you that you may not like. When you were a child, you played without the enemies of play-fullness having much of a presence in your life. You naturally discovered how to play, for it is linked to brain development and how you engage an ever-expanding reality. You were created to play so as to relax, to experience emotional release or restoration, to foster confidence, to engage in relationships with others, or to reconnect after relationships became strained, to anticipate a changed future, and to learn complex problem-solving skills. Those babbling sounds you made as a baby and that you find so adorable in infants helped you to discover sounds, which later became language. Now you write poems and sing karaoke. In the repetitive play of rolling and crawling you discovered how to walk. Playing peek-a-boo with your parents taught you that you would be fine even if your parents were not in sight. You also learned that what disappears returns to you, lovingly engaging you at that time. Through imaginative play with blocks and other toys, you received the foundations for writing, arithmetic, creativity, envisioning, and even empathy.

Playing with toys also developed your dexterity and prepared you for tasks such as driving a car or typing on a keyboard. Physical play developed your muscles and assured that you have a fit body. You continued to engage in self-initiated play long before conscious play was present. Later, playground play taught you how to socialize with others. All along, complex neurological, emotional, relational, and cognitive processes allowed you to play in more advanced ways continually instilling purpose and meaning in your life.

In your preteen years — ages seven to twelve — you began to use specialized tools in your play that you mastered through practice. Maybe you picked up a guitar or another musical instrument and joined the marching band. Or you started playing tennis or, like me, cricket. You participated in a sport or learned music or did cheerleading. As your sense of competence increased, so too did your self-assurance and sense of accomplishment. In these activities, you possibly first experienced the importance of competition, performance, and excellence, dynamic forces and expectations that often take the fun out of any activity. Through your participation in team sports, however, you learned about self-sacrifice, camaraderie, and belonging to a group other than your family, all roots to being a hospitable play-full self. You became disappointed when injuries kept you from playing or when you or your team lost a match or game. Suddenly play became work and practice took up too much time. At that point, you may not have excelled at competition and instead became a supporter of others at play.

As a teen you discovered the joy of participating in culture and you played on the theater stage or attended music concerts. As your emotional maturity increased, you learned about power and control. Your peer group, which became important to you, determined not only your sense of belonging, but also what activities you would like to engage in. As a teen you also experienced the excitement that comes through adventurous play and risk taking. There is a part of us that can be irresponsible, that seeks excitement and rarely dialogues with the part of us that engages in mature, reasoned discernment. Of course, a life ruled by the exciting part has significant elements of risk and is dangerous, even life-threatening. Despite the importance of the peer group, your teen years were also filled with solitary play and the play of courtship and sexuality. Solitary play took you into your room with "Do not disturb" messages and a room (or your ears) filled with music warning your parents and family members to keep their distance. Courtship became a game you often lost, but a game you continued to play — the electricity of your first kiss staying with you, even to this day.

Learning the game of sexuality, you discovered, was pleasurable even if it was confusing. For many it is a painful discovery as the disowned sides of others touched or even wounded your body and life. In your solitary play, the dangers of compulsive play became real. If you are male, masturbation was a practice that probably instilled many guilt feelings. Or you played with the acne on your face or with mind-altering substances. If you are female, maybe you played with food in disturbing ways in an effort to be as skinny as the role models society offered you. Or you played with razor blades that could cut your skin. As teens, we desire to be recognized by the "in" group. So maybe you spent too much time playing video games, or you played sexual games and discovered that such games are best played if one is emotionally, relationally, and spiritually mature, an elusive state for teenagers.

It was during your teenage years that you learned that work is more acceptable than play. As you prepared yourself for further education or a career, you had to assess if you could afford all the time you spent at play. Parents and teachers encouraged you to study more. Inevitably, you made choices that communicated that you knew that work and play cannot coincide and that few people — only the most gifted athletes and artists — have the privilege of making play their work.

By the age of eighteen, you had probably lost your sense of play and, de facto, your play-fullness. You may be one of the lucky few if the play you discovered in your childhood and youth stayed with you into adulthood. For most of us, however, parental and societal or cultural forces and messages either greatly diminished or distorted our sense of play-fullness. When we experience inner turmoil and stress even now as adults, for example, we tend to revisit earlier forms of play that might be risky or repetitive or ritualized.

Philosopher Al Gini writes in his book *The Importance of Being Lazy: In Praise of Play, Leisure, and Vacations* that during the past two decades, children have lost twelve hours of free play a week, including eight hours of unstructured play and outdoor activities. At the same time organized sports have doubled, and spectator sports, *excluding* television, have increased fivefold. *When was the last time you saw a child engaged in free play on television?* Most often children are portrayed as high-achieving mini-adults preoccupied with performance, relationships, or some kind of personal or family dysfunction, such as school problems or divorce. Whether it is *Bob the Builder* or *SpongeBob SquarePants*, work is honored and play is absent.

Despite the fact that children today have more toys than any previous generation, they are not more play-full. These toys are most often sensational, electronic, and skill-oriented in nature (*Jumpstart Baby, Leapfrog Products, Xbox, PlayStation,* and *Wii*), or they are character toys (*Barbie* or *Bratz* dolls, action figures like G.I. *Joe* and *Pokémon*). Sometimes toys are educational in nature, promising better performance and productivity in later years (*Baby Einstein* products such as *Baby Mozart* music). Researchers argue for a strong correlation between the lack of play in the lives of children in particular and the fact that 20 percent of children today have significant emotional, behavioral, and developmental needs that are not met by family, school, or other institutions created to assist in the formation and well-being of children. *Today's children might be the first generation that is less healthy than their parents.*

A poorly developed ability to play affects our lives in significant ways. One effect is that the sense of physical and perceptual mastery we receive from normal play eludes us. Companies like Bell Labs and Intel that hire the best of the best from the best schools find that these bright minds cannot solve problems, for in their drive to get all A's and perfect SAT scores, their new employees never played! With little capacity for play, our capacity for self-initiation, innovation, and creativity, or our ability to engage in collaborative social relationships diminishes. Even our reasoning is affected, making us vulnerable to simplistic, linear, and dichotomous thinking that turns the world into a place easily understood where rights and wrongs rule. With a lack of play in our lives we are arguably more stressed and carry more anxiety than any previous generation. Accompanying the higher levels of anxiety, we also experience higher levels of aggression. It is no surprise that as our play diminished, we invented aggressive spectator sports such as wrestling and ultimate cage fighting.

Discover your history as a play-full person:

+ What is your first conscious memory of yourself being play-full?

+ What messages about play-fullness (or play) have you received?

+ As a child, what were the primary forms of play-fullness you engaged in?

+ When have you felt free to do and be what you choose?

+ When did play-fullness diminish in your life?

+ What corrupted and destructive forms of play have you (or do you) engage in?

+ What freedom have you received through being play-full?

+ What forces inhibit a sense of play-fullness in your life?

+ How are you play-full today?

+ What meaning and purpose does play-fullness have in your life?

+ As you look at your play history, what thoughts and feelings come to mind?

The ways family and society formed us and continue to shape us and the changing world of play lead to play becoming corrupted. Most of us reached a stage in life where playing was discouraged and became fused with guilt. We received messages that playing is wasting time or that working is more important. Maybe you were not allowed to go out to play until you had completed your homework, even if that play would have been free play of creating games on a trampoline or exploring the backyard woods. Some of us even received the message that play is sinful, especially if one wanted to hang out with friends or swim on Sunday, or if one found something hilarious in church and could not stop laughing. Those deriding play-fullness, however, communicate more than the importance of production and work. In this chapter I identify six powerful forces that keep us from being playful, forces we succumb to consciously and unconsciously. When these forces gain control over our lives, we become isolated, bored, frustrated, angry, even depressed and anxious. This desperate place makes us vulnerable to obsessive, addictive, and competitive forms of solitary play such as playing with food (eating disorders), playing with images (pornography and mindless web-surfing), and playing to win (feeling like a loser). The result of corrupted play is always a diminished sense of self, a self that cannot be play-full.

The core enemies of play-fullness are: *criticism, control, compulsion, competition, conflict,* and *consumption.*

Criticism: An Enemy of Play

Hailey's dad was critical of her performance and by being critical he could not communicate to his daughter any affirmation or praise. In fact, Hailey did not pass the ball because she could run circles around her opponents! She was already a gifted soccer player. Like Hailey, most of us grew up with criticism around us. Somehow our parents and teachers believed that by showing us early on what we have done "wrong" or by telling us that we are "inadequate," we would naturally internalize the "good" and become "better." Rarely, however, does criticism lead to positive growth, for as children we cannot distinguish between our sense of self and our work, performance, or behavior.

As an educator, I teach current and future pastoral leaders how to do brief pastoral counseling. Initially, most of these students are poor listeners. They use too many words by giving mini-sermons filled with advice and moral lessons. Like many leaders, they are talking when they should be listening. Over the years, I have discovered that the best approach to help students become effective caregivers is to say something like this: "Your best moment in the role-play was that moment where you sustained the silence and I could see you resisted the urge to speak. That was well done. Do initiate more such moments in your next role-play." This approach is much more effective than previous attempts where I asked students why they use so many words, or whether they were aware of the anxiety in them that fueled their advice giving. Studies confirm that people learn faster when praised compared to being shown their mistakes.

Criticism does not invite mistakes to become our teacher. Rather, we internalize criticism as a critical voice, an *inner critic* that constantly reminds us that we are not good enough, that others will discover us for the fraud we are, or that we should have had that perfect comeback in the moment and not an hour after it was needed. Our ability to internalize relationships, to say that Jesus lives in our heart, for example, means that from an early age we internalize the patterns of relationship and communication we receive. Those early internalizations have a lasting effect on us. Think a minute about the biblical leader Moses. Picked up among the river reeds, Moses reenters his parents' house for a few years in early childhood. Then he is off to Pharaoh's palace. The faith and learning Moses received in his parents' house had much more influence on him than all the privilege and power he had with Pharaoh. One cannot help but wonder what messages Hailey's dad received in his childhood.

> Rather than listening to your inner critic, respond with your *inner innovator,* that part of you that allows you to be creative in life.

The inner critic is the internalization of all the negative comments we heard from parents and other caregivers, teachers, preachers, other authority figures, and even from the silent and skinny models on magazines or television. The inner critic's sole purpose is to criticize our actions, especially activities initiated by our two other parts, the mature self that discerns and the exciting self that takes risks and seeks excitement. When our inner critic is active, we easily criticize others. If that voice reminds you that you are "ugly" or "stupid" and that others are likely to reject you for those reasons, the potential of you finding another person "ugly" or "stupid" is large. Your critic might even tell you that thinking of yourself as a garden that needs to be cultivated is childish! Or that warning a loved one of your destructive traits is a sign of weakness.

Peter grew up on a farm in North Dakota and knows a life of internal and external criticism. Now in his fifties, he remembers his twelfth year and the day his perfectionist father asked Peter to help him cultivate. Peter remembers the excitement he experienced when his father said that he needed Peter's help, for his father was constantly working and was slow to ask for help. Peter went into the field that day and cultivated. Later in the day his father went and looked at Peter's work. When he returned, he informed Peter that he had taken out quite a few soybeans along with the weeds and that it was now too late to replant the beans. His father never again asked Peter for help. Being exposed as unreliable by his father has affected Peter in painful ways. Since that day, Peter said, his inner critic tells him that he cannot be depended upon and that others will be disappointed in his work. In response, Peter says, he resists accountability and working collaboratively and is prone to procrastination.

One way to increase play-fullness within you is to invite your inner critic into a dialogue rather than take a beating from it.

Remember, the inner critic is only one of three parts to our self: You also have a mature, wise part, often called the central self, which remains calm under pressure, engages the inner critic in dialogue, weighs different options, and is caring and empathic toward self and others. A third part of you seeks excitement. This part does not follow any moral or ethical codes and is not necessarily interested in our well-being. Its sole purpose is to seek fun and meet our desires. It is the part of you that seeks the thrill of bungee jumping or zorbing or other activities where you sign your life away before they allow you to participate. Rolling down a hill inside an air-filled ball is an adventure with an element of danger!

Reflect on your inner critic:

+ What does your inner critic tell you?
+ When is the voice most active?
+ Whose voices did you internalize and now hear as your own?
+ How can you engage your inner critic in dialogue the next time it tells you that you are not measuring up to an unnamed standard?

It is this exciting part of him that got King David into trouble. There he is, this man of God and the king of Israel, standing on the roof of his palace when he sees beautiful Bathsheba bathing. Instead of listening to his wise self, which probably told him: "Do not look, David." She is someone else's wife and you already have many! David followed his exciting self. I hear that part of him saying: "David, she's beautiful. Look at her curves and the color of her skin. You'll enjoy having sex with her...." And so David was crafty and got hold of Bathsheba. He became a murderer by arranging for Bathsheba's husband to be killed in battle, and he took Bathsheba as his wife. Despite David's having a contrite heart and praying a beautiful prayer of confession, this event led to the unraveling of David's family. Shortly after David took Bathsheba, his son Amnon rapes (took) his half-sister, Tamar, while David remained a distant, silent, father. Taking revenge, David's son

Absalom took Amnon's life and promptly took on his father's armies. Absalom also dies a violent death. Following our exciting self in unbridled fashion is dangerous and often leads to aggression and violence!

Like the circus artist who straddles two horses running in a wide circle, your mature self within you needs to be in constant dialogue with both your inner critic and your exciting part. The wise self reasons and dialogues with the inner critic and with the exciting part saying: "I am a bit overweight, so from now on I am going to be more mindful about how much food I eat and I'll increase my exercise." Or "seeing if this car can reach 120 mph might be fun, but also dangerous, so I'll not do this on a public road, but instead sign up for a track day where such speeds are possible with relative safety." When you dialogue with your critic and your exciting part, play-fullness is possible. The exciting part of you, in collaboration with the wise part, for example, may sign you up for community theater even though your inner critic tells you that you should not fool yourself into thinking you are an actor!

Dialogue with your inner critic.

Kanisha has a story similar to Peter's on the farm, yet it is different. She was eleven and physically maturing faster than her friends. As her body changed, she gained weight. Her mother, while the family was eating a mashed potato and gravy dish one day, said: "You cannot have that. You are getting too big. Eat your salad!" Kanisha heard this as: "You are fat." Though her dad just sat there, Kanisha felt that his eyes were saying the same thing. Kanisha desperately wanted to be thin to show her mom that she is not fat, but instead over time ate herself into being more than a hundred pounds overweight. Feeling isolated with her low self-confidence and poor body image, she had a slew of relationships in which boyfriends and men used her only to discard her when they were done. She did not care for her body, and they didn't either. Her inner critic would tell her she was dumped because she was fat. Today she dialogues with her inner critic constantly telling herself: "As a big-boned person I'll never be skinny. But I do need to eat healthily and I can make good choices." Kanisha has lost eighty pounds over the past two years by reigning in her inner critic, letting her wise, mature self help her choose foods, and by not letting her exciting part go wild at the buffet.

What shaming experiences have you experienced from critical others? How did your inner critic assimilate those incidents and other similar experiences?

Our relationship with God also becomes tinged with criticism. You may *know* that God is love, slow to anger, and has abundant love to share, as the Psalmist and the prophet Joel write. Your *experience* of God, however, is that God is a punitive father-figure that is taking careful note of all you have done wrong and will punish you severely. God to you is a judging eye!

Jordan and Stephanie are in a painful place. Married a few years, they would love a family of their own. The couple has no problem getting pregnant, but Stephanie has experienced early pregnancy loss three times already. Each miscarriage is heart-wrenching and brings more distance between Stephanie and Jordan. Stephanie feels she is failing Jordan and that her body is betraying her, despite her ob/gyn telling Stephanie that she has a normal, fully functioning body. When the couple is alone, they wonder whether God is punishing them for being sexually active before they were married. They started dating in college and became sexually active almost immediately. Jordan was also sexually active with a few other partners before he met Stephanie.

The inner critics of Stephanie and Jordan have projected the criticism and animosity they hold onto God, who they imagine is now critical and hostile toward them.

When in your life does God become
a punitive authority figure, critical of
who you are and what you do?

The path to play-fullness always includes an encounter with the criticism we received and now freely give to ourselves and also to others. When our inner critic touches our self-esteem, we often end with low self-confidence or poor self-esteem. To protect ourselves against this painful situation, we criticize others or sometimes hide behind a piety that tends to spiritualize everything so that we need not deal with relationships and reality. Defensiveness and denial, however, do not cultivate play-fullness, but awaken another enemy of play: control.

Control: An Enemy of Play

Play-fullness instills a sense of mastery and freedom as persons enter or exit moments of play. When play becomes corrupted, however, we often end with *control*. Hailey's dad not only criticized, he also communicated: "You *must* do X and do it in this manner!" He wanted to control his daughter who, at age six, probably does not even have a firm grasp of what soccer is all about. Outward control, however, is almost always a sign of inward control gone awry. It is a defensive posture, a way of being that might be appropriate in select moments, but not as a general stance in life.

Frank is proud of himself. He sees himself as a person who has his emotions firmly under control. The problem, however, is that he sometimes loses control, and often when least expected. Driving to work the other day, he was listening to the radio when someone abruptly cut into the lane in front of him. The two vehicles nearly collided. In a flash of rage Frank cursed at the other driver and for a few seconds he stayed right on the bumper of the other car flashing his lights and honking his horn. The depth of this road rage surprised even Frank, as sanity slowly returned and he backed off. Frank has his emotions firmly under control until they show up in volcano-like eruptions. When that happens, of course, his inner critic has a field day and makes him feel bad for days, for the inner critic does not forget such a betrayal of self.

> Who or what in life do you have to control? Your weight? A bad habit? A partner? The children? Your emotions? A clean house? Empower yourself to give up some of your control needs.

Control in our lives often takes one of two forms: either we feel we have no control or we feel we need total control. Both of these stances, however, lead to heightened anxiety in our lives. Soon, we discover that "should," "must," and "ought to" language dominates our thoughts and speech. This need to control further leads us to *draw invalid conclusions* and to *predict behavior*. Phil and Yolanda have a difficult relationship with their three-year-old daughter, Megan. They describe her as "feisty" and as having "a will of her own." They say: "We must find a way to make her listen to us. If she is this disobedient as a three-year-old, imagine what it is going to be like when she is a teenager!" Megan, of course, has many years of growth and socialization left before reaching her teen years. If one definition of health is being three at the age of three, and three-year-olds enjoy their growing independence with a sense of will, then Megan is a healthy, normal, three-year-old. To predict that Megan will be a "difficult" teenager is unfair to Megan and brings unwanted anxiety into Phil and Yolanda's parenting.

Phil and Yolanda also *generalize*, telling themselves and all willing to hear: "Every parent struggles with a three-year-old." Drawing invalid conclusions and making gross generalizations induces much stress in our lives and diminishes the potential locked in play-full relationships. As Phil and Yolanda think in terms of right/wrong, black/white, this/that, total obedience/no obedience, their *dichotomous thinking* denies them any possibility of a quality relationship with their daughter. Furthermore, they miss altogether Megan's spirited nature, her liveliness, and the formation of her own voice, all things they could celebrate and encourage.

Think of a difficult situation in a more complex way, resisting the urge to predict behavior or to generalize or to think in dichotomous terms.

Control speaks of distrust in ourselves and in others and leads to the overprotection, overinvestment, overscheduling, and over-programming of our lives and particularly the lives of our children. Whether it is parental control, educational control, government control, control by the peer group, or control by the media, it seems as if our children are constantly pushed and pulled by numerous forces to assure they grow up to be healthy citizens. To be a child is to be enforced! However, such children rarely mature into play-full adults who are imaginative and responsive to life's challenges. Play-fullness brings freedom and spontane-ity, a creative approach to life absent in moments where control reigns. The tension and anxiety that come when play-fullness is corrupted by control rob us of the benefits of play-fullness such as merrymaking, accomplishment, or even peace.

Competition: An Enemy of Play

Play has not escaped the arenas of Rome where winners were worshiped and losers were killed. Many people live by the mottos of Coach Vince Lombardi: "Winning isn't everything; it is the only thing" and, "Winning may not be everything, but wanting to win is!" Whether it is zone soccer, a spelling bee, a NASCAR oval, a football stadium, the baseball diamond, the high-stakes poker table, or the Xbox or PlayStation or Wii hooked up to a high definition television, competition in the United States is thriving. Winning or losing, experiencing success or failure, and making it or not, seem to be the guiding principles of our day. The only trait that outshines the diversity embodied by the American people might be our competitiveness. In today's world, however, competition, or supporting a winner, has a different purpose: It serves a poorly defined self who becomes someone only in winning. That poorly defined self will go to great lengths to win as the drug scandals in major league sports indicate. As such, winning itself is a drug of choice, for if we are winning, it changes the way we feel about ourselves.

Lyle is a poor loser. It started in early childhood. His parents tell him that as early as age five he would get very angry if he lost a game of snakes and ladders. In his anger he would take the board and throw it upside down, effectively ending the game for everyone who was playing. Later, in high school, Lyle made the varsity tennis team and would break a few rackets each season by whacking the ground after serving a double fault or when a line call did not go his way. He also lost a few tennis matches for cursing at an umpire. Competition followed him to college. Feeling uncertain whether he would be able to write "great" term papers in college, he resorted to an online company that guaranteed a plagiarism-proof paper at a price. Now an adult, Lyle admits that his drive to win or to be perceived as the best comes at a cost to his friendships. He started a Friday poker night at his house, but he discovered that many people did not return a second time. He wonders whether his proposal to raise the opening bid from $1 to $5 had something to do with it. He also had an argument with Joe, who he thought was cheating.

What messages of "winning" or "losing" have you received in life? Who do you perceive as winners? Who are the losers?

Lyle's testimony is a far cry from thousands of persons who run marathons or do triathlons just to compete or to finish. Winning is not on their mind, but participation and enjoyment is, as is personal accomplishment. Identifying competition as an enemy of play-fullness recognizes this kind of competition as healthy and needed in life. When play-fullness becomes corrupt and begins to undermine a life of vitality, competitiveness takes on a different form that is easily recognized in our society.

One difference, then, between healthy competition and competition as a corrupt form of play is how rules are viewed. Competition that has become corrupted has no regard for rules and regulations. Any transgression, it seems, is in order as long as it increases the possibility of winning. Healthy competition, as would be true for play-fullness, knows that rules and boundaries are needed to assure the well-being of all and to increase enjoyment. The rules of God, also called the Ten Commandments and the Greatest Commandment, function in a similar manner. They are not meant to inhibit life, but actually to allow life to thrive.

Competition is inherent to all play behavior, as we live life with a sense that "something is at stake." It is thus no surprise that play behavior is often connected to winning. We play for something — participation, accomplishment, even satisfaction — but also to win. Winning is about showing oneself to be superior, a need cultivated in us by society. We want to experience the satisfaction that we did something well, and doing something well means that we are better than others. Sometimes, as for the marathon runners I've mentioned and for many well-known athletes, competition itself is not the driving force, but rather honor, esteem, and praise.

> Find a way to compete where winning does not determine success.

The Latin word for "competition" is *competere*. It means "to seek together." Somehow, we have lost the meaning of *seeking together*, but what we do seek is security or belonging or material goods. We interpret win as "first," "best," or "perfection." "To lose" stems from the Greek *luein*, meaning "to release, to set free, to detach." To be a loser is to be freed, which is countercultural to today's understanding, for we engage in positional competition, which always means that someone is first and best and second is not good enough. It is no surprise that competition often calls in allies such as domination, aggression, and violence, resulting in feelings of alienation and even isolation.

> Identify one activity that gives you a sense of freedom and does not come at the cost of someone else or nature. Engage in that activity often.

We all know stories of the young protégé in one sport or another. Her parent, most often the father, recognizes something special in his child, and then goes on an aggressive path to build a champion. Schooling is replaced with strenuous exercise, and a reward and punishment system is used to encourage the young star to rise. The star does rise, but often at the cost of personal wholeness and the ability to be in a healthy relationship with self and others. Inevitably estrangement from the overbearing parent is reported in the media, and our star searches for a surrogate family that will heal the wounds of her youth. Most often our star's personal life is chaotic and filled with tension and lack of intimacy.

Empower someone to grow toward play-fullness by letting go of the "power over" the person you have. What would "power with" that person look like?

In a world with diminishing resources, competing with others and even with nature has become our way of life. We maintain this life at great cost to ourselves, others, and certainly at great cost to the environment. To be or to feel like a winner as individuals or as a society most often requires corruption, dishonesty, excess, exploitation, greed, power, and violence. Sadly, a life and world without these adversaries is difficult to imagine. Unhealthy competition, however, leads to zero sum situations, where one person or group winning means another person or group loses. Nature, it seems, always loses. One author writes that competition with nature is a misnomer since competition implies some sort of comparability of competitors.

Sometimes competition takes on the form of *perfectionism,* which is closely related to another enemy of play-fullness, compulsion. Perfectionism almost always assures that play-fullness is diminished or even prevented. *Perfectionism is a form of competition against the self in which the self loses every time.* Purely driven by internal forces, but strengthened by external forces, we need no one to compete against. Do not confuse perfectionism with excellence, which is doing your best or striving to reach your potential. Excellence is always mindful of abilities and gifts, of place and time. Perfectionism, however, does not discern. It is a pervasive force that permeates your life, and like competition, it offers the promise of a better self while working in conjunction with your inner critic.

> How does your perfectionism manifest itself? Take a minute and have a short conversation with your perfectionist self.

Ruth feels lonely and isolated. She does not see herself as a competitive person, yet she is in constant battle with her performance, and this causes her much shame, disgust, and self-alienation. The perfectionism permeates her whole life. As a student, she suffered great anxiety when she had to present something in class or when she wrote a paper. She would visit the professor ahead of time, ask advice, hand in drafts, and ask for rewrites. Yet she always ended up with a sense that she did not reach her potential, that she could have achieved a higher grade or that she should have seen better results for the amount of work she put into her presentation. So she convinced herself that she was simply not good enough and did not meet her own internal standards. That she was an above-average student went unnoticed to her and could not bring her satisfaction and self-affirmation. When she paints, an activity she actually enjoys, she rarely completes the painting, for as she continues, she tells herself that it will not resemble the internal image she has in her mind, so it's better to start a new painting. Even in her intimate life, Ruth finds that her perfectionism ruins every relationship. Every time she dates a partner she is soon discouraged, for the flaws she sees in him brings her doubt and anxiety. While dating one person she inevitably meets someone else she feels would be a "better" partner for her, and soon the tension she brings into her current relationship leads to estrangement. Now, in her early thirties, Ruth feels like a "loser," somebody destined to live life alone. "My apartment is a mess, my life is a mess. . . . Pretty much everything is a mess," Ruth says.

> Live with the tension of being
> good enough, for it does not seek
> perfectionism and it resists mediocrity.
> What would it look like for you to
> be a good enough partner or spouse?
> Imagine yourself being a good enough
> parent or good enough employee.

Healthy competition maintains a strong sense of mutuality among competitors. Where competition has become a corrupted form of play, mutuality is replaced by apathy and distance-inducing tension in relationships. In such moments, competition does not support the fruit of a play-full life — peace and justice. Winning is primarily interested in the allocation of resources, whereas a play-full person asks: *Who am I?* and *Who are you?* and *Who are we together?* As you discern the answers to these questions, winning and losing cease to make sense. A play-full person certainly can be competitive, but not in a desperate attempt to feel better or to become someone in winning even if it comes at the cost of others. The self-acceptance and other-acceptance inherent to play-fullness keep competition from becoming something needed to strengthen a weak and insecure self.

Play-fullness finds enjoyment in healthy competition. Competition, according to the Greek philosopher Plato, is best understood in terms of *completion, coordination,* and *cooperation.* Commit to these values and your play-fullness will increase. Corrupt forms of competition rarely portray traits such as completion, coordination, and cooperation, but may awaken another enemy of play-fullness: compulsion.

> Imagine asking a friend or loved one: *Who are we together?* Envision asking that also of the child laborer or woman in Asia or elsewhere stitching your next pair of expensive sneakers.

Compulsion: An Enemy of Play

Monk, as you may know, is a well-known television detective despite the 312 fears, compulsions, and phobias of the main character, Adrian Monk, played by actor Tony Shalhoub. As I write this book, *Monk* is in its final season. In the opening show of the series, Monk has to interrupt his detective work to rush home because he is convinced he left the stove on. Walking down the street, he touches and counts every parking meter he passes, and he then finds it impossible to enter an elevator because a coughing woman has awakened his fear of getting sick. Later, a murderer moves past him on a ladder because Monk is paralyzed by his fear of heights. As a television show, *Monk* is doing much to show not only how restrictive obsessions and compulsions are, but also how one overcomes compulsion.

When play-fullness become hyperplay or overplay and takes the form of *compulsion,* with its repetitive thoughts, images, impulses, behaviors, or mental acts, it has lost its life-giving properties that are performed to relieve anxiety or distress. Compulsion is repetitive play. Someone with a compulsive trait is preoccupied with details or rules or order or control; or the person may exhibit perfectionism that interferes with task completion; or show rigidity and stubbornness; or the person is inflexible and over-conscientious. Some persons with compulsions hoard objects with no sentimental or economic value, while others have somatic concerns. All compulsions serve a single purpose: they reduce anxiety. Play-fullness too reduces tension. Compulsions, however, describe a type of bondage to your inner anxieties with one more round of repetition that awaits you.

What habits or rituals do you have that remove anxiety but diminish your life?

Myra is addicted to her BlackBerry. Or to be more specific, she is addicted to texting her friends, reading her email or the tweets she receives from friends on *Twitter*, checking up on the status of the hundreds of people on her *Facebook* wall, and playing some of the applications she has downloaded. She has had several close calls driving her car while on her BlackBerry, both with other vehicles and almost running off the road. Myra jokingly calls rumble strips her best friends! At a recent lunch meeting, a girlfriend gave her an ultimatum: "Put down your BlackBerry and talk to me or assume this will be our last lunch together." She put her phone away, but she sensed an urge in her to rush the lunch so that she could check up on the nearly five hundred emails, tweets, and notices she receives every day. Myra is not recognizing that she has isolated herself from all her friends, spending most of her evenings with her computer on her lap and her phone in her hand. "Pull yourself away from that *iPhone* and read this story," the *newspaper* article read. With her nose close to a small bright screen, Myra never received the invitation to revisit her relationship with technology.

Abraham does not carry a Smartphone, but he is a driven individual. Always struggling with his weight, he accepted the challenge from a friend to sign up for a mini-triathlon. Abraham was hooked. Barely able to finish his first race, he started practicing and has now completed twenty-seven full triathlons. He practices running before work, and after work he swims laps at the local aquatic center. Sometimes over lunch he will do weight training. On weekends he spends a lot of time in the saddle going on long bicycle rides. He feels he needs to do this to gain some mastery in a very competitive sport. Abraham's wife, Zeta, tries to understand, but finds it difficult to support him. They spend very little time together and their intimate life has dwindled, partly because they are rarely awake at the same time. Like Myra, Abraham seems unable to recognize the cost of his passion on his marriage. The interpersonal conflict they experience as they maintain their compulsion does not seem to bother them in any way.

> How might you change your relationship with technology — televisions, computers, and cell phones, for example — to support your play-full life?

In a world where we are controlled by numerous outside forces and where uncertainty is the only sure thing, compulsions give us a sense of control and certainty. They also function as a primary source for seeking tension release. Like many persons with a compulsive trait, Myra and Abraham find it difficult to express deep emotion such as warmth and tenderness, while they have no difficulty expressing anger, frustration, and irritability. Their employers, however, appreciate and even reward their industriousness, ambition, and ability to focus. Both of them are driven, but being driven is rarely life-giving for a lengthy period of time. One cannot sustain it beyond a number of days, for drivenness speaks more to anxiety than the direction of your actions. Of course, the thought of repeating a behavior for a number of times that has significant, even magical, value — such as three, four, seven, or even forty — sounds freeing. There are reasons why we do not choose 52 or 365: we know we would not be able to sustain such a lengthy time of anxiety and they do not sound magical or spiritual!

Do not answer your cell phone if you do not have time for a meaningful conversation. Or, switch off your cell phone's notification system so as not to become a slave to a blinking LED or small icon.

Whoever *must* play, cannot be play-full. The Hebrew word for salvation, *yashah*, basically means creating space, making room, or being without compulsion. Not everyone may associate with the particular extreme forms of overplay Myra and Abraham engage in. Nonetheless, there are many forms of overplay that you and I do engage in, and they all diminish our play-full lives:

- Corey spends much time in his shop, tinkering with this and that. Retreating into his shop is especially precious and comes naturally when there is tension in the house, such as recently when Corey's wife tried to tell him that she needs him to partake more in the household chores and parenting the kids.

- Dora soothes herself. Returning from work, she feels a hunger growing in her. This hunger is tied to feeling a sense of belonging. If her two teenage children are home when she arrives, the hunger disappears, but if she comes home to an empty house, she finds herself eating salty snacks within seconds. She cannot stop this unhealthy habit. At times she purges the snacks she has just consumed.

- Yuri has a high need of order and neatness. He ascribes it to his days in the military. His clothes and shoes are neatly ordered in his walk-in closet and his socks and underpants are color coordinated in separate drawers. His shirts hang exactly two inches apart with dark shirts on the right. His personal need for order has infiltrated his parenting in ways that cause unwanted tension in the house. Yuri and his wife parent a toddler, and at times he is angry with his son, who cannot eat without making a big mess.

• Joanne is recently retired and follows the money markets carefully. She trades in penny stock and constantly finds herself checking up on her investments. Lately, Joanne declined to play afternoon bridge with friends since much action often takes place before the closing of the markets. She does not recognize that she rarely speaks to her friends anymore.

• Ely said it started innocently. He visited image libraries on the Internet but soon that escalated into him needing his "fix" of pornography every day. Trying to avoid computer viruses, he has a paid subscription to an adult website. He had one close call at work recently when someone walked into his office while he was accessing the website on his Smartphone. Ely believes he can engage women as objects on the web without objectifying the women he meets in real life, including his wife.

• Sandra finds that her choice of overplay, keeping the house clean, is brought about by boredom. Whenever she's at home and she has nothing to do, she finds herself cleaning an already clean home. Boredom often brings anxiety and self-doubt, and Sandra is managing those tensions by cleaning. Recently she told someone: "My mom can walk into our house at any time and will not think that I'm a sloppy housekeeper."

• Ray's form of overplay is counting, much like Adrian Monk and his counting of parking meters. Whenever he stops at a red light, he counts the seconds he is "wasting time." Yesterday was a bad traffic day. Barely back with his family, he shared: "I lost eight minutes and forty-two seconds today standing at red lights." He didn't notice that his family was not interested in what he shared nor that he never asked them about their day.

Like all forms of overplay, these compulsions too become an emotional and spiritual dependency that self-perpetuates. They provide their own energies to accelerate. Compulsion makes us a slave of something or it helps us avoid something we should not avoid. Compulsive behavior is not life-giving nor life-sustaining. It may know pleasure, but not delight. Most often it brings tension into our interpersonal relationships as others have to comply with our overplay; tension we then release through our desired choice of overplay. Here there is not much of a difference between compulsion as doing something and procrastination as a form of overplay of doing nothing. Both are common choices to manage anxiety. Of course, all of the compulsions mentioned here can grow into becoming part of an obsessive-compulsive disorder, at which time normal functioning and balance in life is lost. This would be true for 2–3 percent of the general population. Seeking professional help is courageous and freeing if you cannot find peace and freedom on your own.

Identify one activity that offers you delight and not only pleasure. Engage in that activity and share the delight with a loved one, friend, and stranger.

Whereas compulsion is characterized by repetition, play-fullness is characterized by curiosity and experimentation. Since compulsions undermine your well-being, they are a form of aggression toward your self.

Conflict: An Enemy of Play

The prophet Elisha was his play-full self. He was telling the king of Israel where the king of Aram would put up camp. Since Israel was at war with Aram at that time, Elisha's communications to the king of Israel were very helpful. Monarchs, of course, don't take it kindly when their plans are thwarted and Elisha's actions angered the king of Aram. The king's advisors told him that Elisha knows the very words he speaks in his bedroom! What a shocking and scary message that must have been.... So the king of Aram did what kings do. He mobilized his army to capture one old man and his servant boy. The situation would be almost laughable if it were not so serious. As Elisha's servant prepared hot water for his master one morning, he saw them surrounded by an army of horses and chariots. He became fearful and woke his master. Elisha, however, was not fazed one bit. He told the servant boy that those who surround the Arameans are more than the Arameans who encircled the home of Elisha and his servant boy. Utterly confused, the servant boy looked at his master. And so Elisha prayed — a play-full activity in itself — and the eyes of the servant boy were opened to see the hills around them filled with horses and chariots of fire. Seeing entities that reside *between* reality and fantasy is easy for a play-full self!

Engaging the Arameans, Elisha prayed again and the army was struck with blindness. Elisha promptly led them right into Samaria, the capital of Israel, and then prayed again. The eyes of the Arameans were opened and they saw themselves at the mercy of their enemy, the Israelites. Now the king of Israel got really excited about having his enemies in the palm of his hand. With exuberance he asked Elisha: "Shall I kill them, my father, shall I kill them!" Calmly, Elisha answered: "No, do not kill them; give them food and water and let them go." And so the two armies feasted together and the Arameans left. In the Bible this story ends rather abruptly: "So the bands from Aram stopped raiding Israel's territory." Imagine that: making friends through feasting with your enemies! The results of play-fullness!

Killing and violence or eating, drinking, and feasting — the differences between corrupted forms of play and a play-full life. There is an unwanted side to play, which is aggression and violence. As a first grader, my best friend at the time, William, took judo lessons. Whenever he had to practice to test for a new rank and belt, he used me as his sparring partner. I was always game, since I thought I could gain some self-defense moves that might come in handy one day.

As I was thrown this way and that way, and as I was held in place feeling pretty helpless, our sparring became a full-blown fight within minutes. The fight would end when one of us cried or gained a bloodied nose, as happened a few times.

Conflict speaks to any behavior or action, verbal or non-verbal, which physically hurts others or has the potential to cause bodily, emotional, relational, or even economic harm. To speak to your inner critic, as this chapter encourages, also indicates a form of conflict, psychic conflict. This conflict, however, is different from the conflict we've identified as the enemy of play-fullness. The latter causes hurt in you and others as it becomes bullying, spanking, interpersonal violence, and even war, whereas the psychic conflict may lead to play-fullness. Irrespective of how conflict as a corrupt form of play-fullness is manifest, it never creates peace with a sense of justice for your self or for others.

Much of play is built on our aggressive impulses. From our toddler days, but especially as preschoolers, pretend aggressing and play-fighting are part of every person's experience. Rough and tumble play, where parents chase their toddler who stumbles away in "fear," or two preschoolers who push and shove each other, prepares children for an adulthood where they have to reckon with their own aggression and destructive impulses. An excellent example of how children learn the dances of love, hate, fear, and envy, the powerful forces behind most conflict, is to observe how children engage their stuffed animals or soft toys. These objects are lovingly cuddled and then aggressively thrown, trampled, and even mutilated. The latter, of course, indicates the aggressive forces integral to being a human.

Sadly, we live in a culture that encourages aggression more in boys than in girls. This leads to boys growing up overly aggressive and girls being inhibited in their aggression. For most of us, however, our aggression went underground when we reached our teen years. Our aggression became more sophisticated, as it became part of sports such as football, hockey, basketball, volleyball, karate, and a large number of video games. Many children and teens, however, deeply internalized the conflict that shaped them.

Biographers and scholars tell us that the veteran evangelist Billy Graham was severely beaten as a child. Both his parents, evangelists themselves, would beat him, his father with a belt and his mother with a switch. The abuse finally stopped in Graham's teen years after he fought back, kicking his father as he lay on the ground with his father flailing away and Graham breaking his father's ribs in self-defense. Graham was beaten for small transgressions and built a career on telling people that their actions and how they live their lives will have grave consequences.

> How has physical violence touched your life? Imagine God's Spirit tenderly blowing over the fingerprints and footprints left by others on your made-of-dust body.

When we seek intimacy — a play-full activity — and cannot find it, conflict as corrupt play-fullness may enter. That is why the Travis family is hurting. Dad Garrett, working in the manufacturing industry, suddenly finds himself without a job after the company he worked for laid off half of its employees. Mom Imelda works part-time, which helps with the finances. Together they parent three boys, ages seven, nine, and eleven. The boys are busy, feeding off the tension that is in the house. Initial attempts by Garrett to find reemployment have been unsuccessful and he spends most of his days at home, catching up on old sports broadcasts. Last night the couple reached a breaking point. Over dinner,

Imelda and Garrett argued after she experienced him as being too strict with the boys. The next moment Garrett took his glass of water and threw it across the kitchen. As angry words flew back and forth, the boys looked at each other wide eyed. They barely breathed. Imelda tried to explain to the boys that their dad is stressed. The family is unable to restore intimacy and hope in the face of Garrett's job loss.

How might you call on your play-fullness to defuse a situation that can escalate and become conflictual or even violent?

When our play-fullness decreases, the possibility of our using angry words, conflict, and even physical violence increases. I think it is impossible for a play-full person to become violent, even when angry. Being play-full offers many options that all exclude physically or emotionally hurting someone we love or someone we do not even know. Since children would break house rules to receive attention, affirming and recognizing a child — both play-full acts — open new possibilities for those of us who parent or look after children. Feeling disconnected from me after I attended a conference, our youngest daughter became defiant. About to leave the house for a weekend getaway and already behind schedule, she refused to put on her shoes and socks and join her older sister, who was already waiting outside. Recognizing that my wife and daughter were in a stalemate position, each just getting more frustrated with the other, I asked my daughter whether I could carry her upside down to the vehicle. It took her only one second to say, "Yes!" I replied that I'd love to carry her upside down to the vehicle, but that I could do so only if she had her shoes on. She brought her shoes and socks, I helped her put them on, and then carried her, head down, outside. Seeing this spectacle and hearing the laughter, our oldest announced she was going back into the house and also wanted to be carried upside down! Play-fullness offers many opportunities not to resort to verbal or physical conflict in moments of tension or even despair.

Born and raised in South Africa during the heyday of Apartheid, another violent system created by humanity, I have seen and experienced the personal and interpersonal damage done when conflict and violence become dominant players in society. Upon my arrival in the United States in 1993, I found myself in Bridgeport, Connecticut, a city that at that time had more conflict and violence than I ever experienced in South Africa. Working as a chaplain I had to ask Hospital Security to escort me to where my car was parked. At night, shots could be heard. I soon discovered that what I experienced is normal for many inner cities, even today. The American nightmare, fueled by conflict and interpersonal violence, is as prevalent as the American dream.

The physical conflict that is present in our families and cities is also present among nations. We can easily see that conflict and the competitive nature of play-behavior are related in the language we use about the wars the United States is currently engaged in. In our desire to "win" the current wars in Iraq and Afghanistan, we are frustrated when terrorists do not play according to the "rules of the game." We send tanks and battalions; "they" send suicide bombers, some of whom are women and children. I wonder whether our nation could have discovered peace and justice if we had been play-full with our grief after 9/11? If we had written laments, named our unbelief and helplessness, and mourned the dead? What would have happened if we had called on the rest of the world to become significant to us in our loss and hurt? No war has ever been "won." Generations to come will live with the emotional, relational, and spiritual trauma of war. Where past wars stimulated the economy, modern wars may have the opposite effect. It is a sobering thought that every generation in the United States for the past seventy years has experienced a war: World War II, the Korean Conflict, Vietnam, the Gulf War, the Iraq War,

Afghanistan, and the ongoing War on Terror. The War on Terror, due to its ideological nature, can be "won" only when enemies become friends.

Conflict as a corrupt form of play leads to wounded individuals, families, societies, and nations. It also leads to despair and the physical annihilation of lives and buildings and infrastructure. Play-fullness, instead, leads to the destruction of preconceived notions in fantasy. I remember my college years and recognize that most persons of color are not dangerous or communists, as I was led to believe by the Apartheid government and even by the church that nurtured my faith. Destruction of preconceived ideas you may carry in your mind rarely hurts another. Rather, it leads to the discovery of a stranger as a friend.

What preconceived notions do you need to destroy of persons who are a "them" or a "they" or an "issue" or a "lifestyle" for you?

Conflict breeds more conflict and violence, whereas play-fullness teaches us about self-empathy and having compassion and empathy for others. Conflict breeds a sense of mastery fused with turmoil and tension; play-fullness offers mastery with a sense of inner peace and justice.

Consumption: An Enemy of Play

A natural companion to a world in which radical individualism is shaped by forces such as criticism, control, compulsion, competition, and conflict is a sixth enemy of play-fullness, *consumption*. There is a strong correlation between shopping in a materially oriented culture and playing. The marketing industry has succeeded in turning every person, especially children, into a consumer sub-culture. *Consumption speaks to the emotional, spiritual, and relational hunger that we experience and that we seek to satisfy by taking in excessively.* Consumption is a form of gluttony that leaves us with a perpetual desire for more. The irony, of course, is that a play-full life also wants more — closer intimate relationships, for example — but consumption is a vain attempt at seeking wholeness or balance in life.

How would your life change if you managed to reduce your garbage and regular waste by one-third?

We learn a different way of living from the Swedes. *Lagom* is a beautiful Swedish word. Like many words in foreign languages that speak to peace and community and social well-being, *lagom* is too large a concept to translate into a single English word. It speaks to finding balance in your belongings, to having enough. It also speaks to living a life of moderation, to being satiated with what one has, and to working toward a sustainable society. Whether the object of choice is food, shelter, or clothing, *lagom* encourages us to walk in balance between having too much and having too little.

Make a list of the possessions you own but rarely or never use. Shorten that list.

A Judeo-Christian worldview should speak into our consumerist culture, but rarely does. From the manna and quail the Israelites received while wandering in the desert, just enough for every day, to a widow's oil that filtered into her community, to the sad story of a rich young man who chose possessions and wealth above a personal relationship with Jesus, there are many references in the Bible that protest against our consumerist culture. If two things are true about Americans, it would be that we are consumers, and that we are also believers. Singer and songwriter Leonard Cohen captures this paradox in his song "The Land of Plenty" when he sings: "For the millions in a prison, that wealth has set apart; For the Christ who has not risen, from the caverns of the heart."

Choose any object, the apple you eat or the cell phone you use, and trace its path from raw material to finally resting in your hand.

Consumption is an enemy of play-fullness, for it is a form of play that has been corrupted in an affluent world filled with many goods, a world where the gap between rich and poor is getting wider every day. Until the eighteenth century, the word "consumption" was not used as we use it today. Rather, "consumption" was used to describe the depletion and exhaustion of someone who had tuberculosis. This changed in the beginning of the eighteenth century and today "consumer" is a common word describing the buyer or acquirer of material goods. For many the word "consumption" has a negative connotation since consumption threatens the environment, it does not address the plight of the poor and marginalized, and it has become a way to be someone, even if at the cost of someone else.

Consumption says much about our economy, but it says more about our lives and who we are. Psychologists remind us that, if our emotional, relational, and physical needs were not met in adequate ways in early infancy, we develop a self that is very compliant to outside demands. This self is a "hungry," insatiable, or gluttonous self as it seeks ways to be more authentic and feel secure. Consumption is then the "hungry self's" attempt to satiate itself. Due to its very nature, however, no amount of money or goods or even images or web pages satisfy the hunger or instill in us a sense of vitality and aliveness. Of course, if we try to find our identity in work and thus work more hours than is healthy for us or for our intimate relationships, we tend to reward ourselves for that work. Buying is a way to reward ourselves and to change the way we experience ourselves as depleted, stressed-out, overworked, and underappreciated individuals.

How do you integrate your buying habits into the play-full self you are becoming?

Giving examples of how we have become consumers is probably not needed. Our home is probably like yours. In the basement of our home are numerous plastic containers with old computers, cordless phones, PDAs, remote controls, and more. Our clothes closets are filled with enough clothes to wear a new outfit every day of the week, with many days to spare. Branded by media savvy companies, our clothes come with labels burdened by economic injustices such as child labor, poor wages, and dangerous working conditions. Our daughters have more toys than they ever play with. Our house is littered with many small stuffed animals, all having carbon footprints bigger than the footprint of an elephant.

Go through your clothes and belongings and donate items not used during the past two years to a charity in your town.

A play-full life is a life that cares about the environment and as such resists the invitation from society and government alike to become a consumer. As an enemy of play-fullness, consumption is difficult to overcome for it is woven into the very fiber of how our society functions. The price we pay, however, is far reaching, since it affects the vital selves we are.

In Conclusion

The six C's discussed in this chapter are all enemies of a play-full life. As persons of faith, we have a different relationship with our enemies. Jesus told his followers that one should love your enemies. *So how does one "love" criticism and control, or even conflict? How does one "love" compulsion, competition,* and *consumption?* One way to "love" these enemies is to *befriend* them. There might be no better way to keep your enemies close at hand. *Befriending* entails a collaborative relationship between two individuals that involves mutual recognition, knowledge, and respect. It also communicates emotional and even physical closeness and a desire to seek out one another. A play-full self befriends these enemies by constantly recognizing and acknowledging when these forces become present in your life and relationships. By respecting the power that *criticism, control, conflict, compulsion, competition,* and *consumption* have and by respectfully disagreeing with their messages and mannerisms, you minimize the destructive effect of these forces on your life.

What would *befriending* the enemies of
play-fullness look like for you?

Another way to "love" these enemies is to introduce them to even more powerful forces — many already active in your life — that promote a play-full life. These play-full practices I discuss in the next two chapters.

TWO

Play-fullness Practicing (Part 1)

Realness, Creativity, and Boundlessness

Practicing play-fullness? With disbelief but definite curiosity a friend verbalized her surprise about our conversation. Over a cup of coffee for her and *Rooibos* tea for me she pushed me about becoming play-full, particularly when I commented that it takes much practice to become a play-full self. With three young children and a career to nurture, she wondered whether she has time left to practice anything. I had said that practicing play-fullness means loving oneself so that one can love one's neighbor. It speaks to who we are to ourselves and to others, as parents, partners, and professionals. Juggling a few different understandings of the word "practice," I suggested that to "practice" is to work for a time under the guidance of a coach or by yourself; the length of time we spend doing it is less important than the fact that it is a repeated exercise, just as we might practice a specific sport or hobby such as playing piano. But "practice" also means applying a method, as when we put into practice what we have learned. "Practice," I concluded, also speaks to what is customary and expected, as in parenting practices. To practice play-fullness might mean to do something specific, such as dialoguing with your inner critic; or it can be a method, an approach to certain situations; or play-fullness becomes a way of being, at which point it is your practice, your way of relating to the world.

Yes, practicing play-fullness is a paradox. The paradox of play-fullness is that it is a sign of the very core of our *being*, who we are as persons. Yet play-fullness also refers to our *doing* as we engage in various activities. The paradox my friend and I faced was this: Play-fullness is about who we are and not what we do, yet what we do can be play-full! We practice life, knowing that *doing* something is not the same as *being* someone. Since play-fullness is inherent to the core of our beings, my friend's concern of not having time speaks only to one understanding of practicing play-fullness: setting time apart to do something special. I contend that if you are a play-full person, you carry the potential to be play-full in all moments without being conscious of or even burdened by time.

Some children like to read the same book over and over again. When they were younger, my daughters had a few books to which they constantly returned. Even as repetition is important for children as they learn sight words, practice memorization, and find security in the known, it can be a very boring experience for the parent who has to read, yet again, the same familiar book. At least it was for me. Therefore I always gave my daughters choices: I can read the story as is but make mistakes, which they need to catch. Or I can sing the story in one of the languages spoken in our home, a "boy opera" or a "girl opera" or a "country and western" voice, or I can enter into a rap style. Finally, they can "read" the story to me. No matter what they choose, a ritual such as reading before bedtime is suddenly transformed. My daughters often asked for the "opera choice" and then in the best opera voice I could muster, I sang the story to them. Soon they too would join in, singing as low as they could if I was singing in the "boy opera" voice. My daughters also loved it when I read and made mistakes, catching me time and again. Here the play-fullness was an invitation to move the boundaries of our reading and to experience some creativity. I could sense the enjoyment that was awakened in them. Best of all, I loved those moments too!

Not to worry if you don't have young children to read to. Instead, imagine singing out loud the next e-mail you receive or magazine article you read. Surely even imagining it changes your embodied self! After initial anxiety or even resistance, I envision some laughter and even joy coming to you as you decide in what style you will sing and take on this challenge.

Singing, however, is not always possible. In the introduction, Ben showed us that even in a painful moment such as feeling rejected after not receiving a promotion, his play-fullness allowed him to play with time. It allowed him to express self-empathy for this current hurt, yet opened visions of a different future, one where rejection does not determine his self-experience. Likewise, Anna was play-full near the end of her life, naming her fears even as she envisioned what heaven is like. As a state of being, time and place are not major concerns when it comes to being play-full.

This chapter and the next are a unit and together cover six practices of play-fullness. These far-reaching practices — as things you do *and* as ways of being — combined with diminishing the enemies discussed in chapter 1, awaken play-fullness within you and with others. The six practices are: *realness, creativity, boundlessness, slowness, hospitality,* and *transcendence.* This chapter addresses the first three:

- *Realness* challenges you to hold polarities or opposites in close relationship and to resist dichotomous thinking

- *Creativity* invites you to use and nurture your imagination

- *Boundlessness* beckons you to move beyond a life constrained by boundaries and limits, beyond a life that knows only winners and losers, a life of general shortage

All of these practices touch your emotions, your relationships, and your sense of spirituality.

Practicing Realness

Be for real! Many of us have used those exact words to encourage someone else to be different. In more painful moments, we have received those words from someone or a group who disapproved of us at that moment. Sometimes we hear those words when we are experienced as outlandish and others find us difficult to believe. Realness, however, is not a given as much as it is a process. It is possible to be an adult person, advanced in years, yet never having attained realness. The thought that one can be successful in the eyes of the world and yet not achieve realness is a sad thought. Not being real comes at a cost to self and others — a cost rarely calculated.

But what is being real? In Marjorie Williams's classic 1922 book, *The Velveteen Rabbit: Or How Toys Become Real,* we find an answer to this question. In a fascinating conversation between a spotted, brown-and-white Rabbit with real thread whiskers and the Skin Horse, we discover something about play-fullness. The Rabbit was a gift to a boy, who loved the Rabbit for only two hours before moving on to more exciting toys. Put away in the toy cupboard, the more expensive toys had contempt for toys like the Rabbit, for the Rabbit was made of sawdust. The mechanical toys in turn saw themselves as superior to all, for they were full of modern ideas. The Skin Horse lived in the nursery for many years and his brown coat was tattered and in some places his seams showed. A long time ago his tail had been pulled out and was replaced by a string of beads once used as a necklace. Everybody knew that the Skin Horse was wise and so the Rabbit asked the Skin Horse, "What is real?" for he thought to be real you had to have things inside you that buzzed thanks to a stick-out handle. The Skin Horse answered:

> "Real isn't how you are made. . . . It's a thing that happens to you. When a child loves you for a long, long time, not just to play with, but *really* loves you, then you become Real."
>
> "Does it hurt?" asked the Rabbit.
>
> "Sometimes," said the Skin Horse, for he was always truthful. "When you are Real you don't mind being hurt."
>
> "Does it happen all at once, like being wound up," he asked, "or bit by bit?"
>
> "It doesn't happen all at once," said the Skin Horse. "You become. It takes a long time. That's why it doesn't happen

often to people who break easily, have sharp edges, or have to be carefully kept. Generally, by the time you are Real, most of your hair has been loved off, and your eyes drop out, and you get loose in the joints and very shabby. But these things don't matter at all, because once you are Real you can't be ugly, except to people who don't understand."

"I suppose *you* are real?" said the Rabbit. And then he wished he had not said it, for he thought the Skin Horse might be sensitive. But the Skin Horse only smiled.

What does it mean to be real? To be real is the result of being loved, by someone else first and later by numerous others and ourselves. What was true for the Skin Horse is also true for us: we need to be loved by others to thrive. We need to be held in relationships where we grow as individuals, where our rough edges are smoothed over, where we receive vitality. The need to be held and to remain vital never disappears and may actually grow stronger as we age.

> Who first loved you into realness? Find a way to express gratitude to that person or share that same love with someone else.

Besides being loved and held in relationships, practicing realness beckons us to embrace certain polarities inherent to being human. These polarities, in turn, further define what realness really is. Of course, before we embrace these polarities, we need to recognize them as part of who we are. Realness as a practice of play-fullness without self-awareness is elusive. Strangely, realness seems especially natural to preschool children, who seemingly have no difficulty in holding on to the polarities we embody. It is only as we become educated and mature that we lose our realness. Now we have to work hard to reclaim something that once

was natural. The polarities you embrace as you practice realness
include:

+ Being resilient, yet also sensitive and in need

+ Being grounded, yet now and then drifting

+ Celebrating your uniqueness while accepting your
  insignificance

+ Loving others while tolerating your capacity to hate and
  hurt others

+ Being sane but every so often having thoughts that portray
  your insanity

+ Feeling as if you have it "together," yet sometimes also
  feeling as if you are coming unraveled

+ Being responsive to the world, while also carrying much
  capacity for reactivity

+ Contributing to culture and tradition and taking from
  culture and tradition

+ Entering into relationship while also needing to withdraw

+ Remaining real even in moments of feeling unreal

Which of these polarities do you identify
in yourself? Be on the lookout for the
polarities you cannot recognize in
yourself yet.

Because we are made in the image of God, it is no surprise
that we are paradoxical creatures. God, after all, self-portrays as
a loving, caring God, slow to anger and harboring abundant love,
yet also shows anger and judgment that leads to destruction as
nations and people are sentenced to death. In holding polarities,
in being real, we honor our Creator. Conversely, when we buy into

false dichotomies and the creative tension between our opposites disappears, we dehumanize others and ourselves.

Martin and Emma describe it as a "double whammy": within two weeks both of them lost their jobs. Yet the couple seems to be doing okay, experiencing a normal level of anxiety as they ponder options and speak with their financial institutions and other parties of interest. When asked how they are doing, Martin often answers: "I have so little time, so much to do!" Catching his questioner off-guard, Martin continues: "The other day I asked my car's navigation device to take me to a new job and I got lost." Emma would chime in saying that she always thought she was indispensable, being such a great human resource person, but then she discovered to her horror that the company had survived the past weeks without her there. "They never even called me *once* to ask me something!" she says with feigned disbelief. Over dinner one night, the couple wondered whether their computer passwords were still active and what would happen if they were to plant a virus on the networks or delete important files. Emma also imagined that if they could get into the buildings where they had worked they could light a candle under a fire sprinkler and watch as everything is soaked with water. Envisioning scenarios of tremendous chaos among their former colleagues, they laughed and even relaxed. The couple then went to bed knowing that they have no desire to actually follow through on their diabolical fantasies. *Destruction in fantasy can be much more rewarding than destruction in reality!*

At other times Martin and Emma experience despair and deep concern, for both are in mid-career and they know that finding employment will not be easy and might even include retraining, or worse for their teenage kids, relocation. Many of their friends expressed anger at the injustice of it all but also expressed their support by offering to pay for expensive medicine Emma takes for a chronic illness. Accepting the gifts of friends is not easy for Martin and Emma, but they have learned that by receiving the gifts they allow their friends to be gracious toward them. Martin and

Emma are being real in the midst of concern and gratitude. They
are not denying the difficulties they are facing and they know that
difficulties are not problems. Difficulties are those things that happen to us that are most often unpreventable or just plain annoying
and are best solved with commonsense solutions or logical reason.
Problems develop when difficulties are managed poorly or not at
all and represent a deadlock, an impasse, with increased anxiety and dysfunction. Problems are much more troublesome and
resistant to change than are difficulties. Furthermore, Martin and
Emma recognize that adjustments in their lifestyle, such as can-
celing satellite television, not eating out, and curbing credit card
purchases are not failures of some sort, but may even be healthy
for them as a family.

Identify one difficulty in your life that,
unless engaged in a play-full way, has
the potential to become a problem.

When we practice realness and hold the polarities of our existence, we awaken realness in others. As Martin became play-full
with the tensions he experienced, he awakened play-fullness in
Emma. Engaging paradox always demands of us some sense of
inner security, for it brings tension to our selves. Without a sense
that we hold the tension, we'll attempt to collapse the polarity
to one side or the other, fueling a dualistic worldview of good
and bad, right and wrong, us and them. So too we place ourselves at risk of "spilling over" as our anxiety leaves our bodies
and enters the bodies of others, most often our partners and
our children. Gossip is a great example of spilling over. When
juicy bits of information we possess infuse us with tension, we
are at risk of "spilling over" by telling people who should not
be told. Whenever we gossip we are unreal and most often we

dehumanize others and ourselves. When our personhood or part-nering becomes strained, spilling over can be more dangerous. The tension within and between parents spills over into the chil-dren who suddenly offer mom and dad vague but real pain, often a stomachache. Or a child suddenly becomes asthmatic as the tension fills her lungs. Sometimes the tension spills over into fam-ilies in deadly ways, and we hear of another family experiencing a murder-suicide. How often do we hear of a teenager taking a gun to school or someone using an assault weapon in the workplace or in a church, leaving death and despair in their wake? Spilling over, especially in violent ways, most often hurts someone.

Imagine you have a container large enough — a secure, roomy inner space — to hold whatever tension you experience. Find appropriate relationships to process the tension you hold.

To hold our paradoxical existence, we need space inside like the bison of the plains of Wyoming. We also need persons around us who love us deeply, preferably play-full persons who have achieved realness themselves and who have a significant relationship with their polarities. The Skin Horse had it right when he told the Rabbit that realness is birthed in the quality of one's relation-ships. Achieving realness is not effortless or painless, for you enter unknown territory as you enter into your own depths. Sometimes realness actually costs money as we enter into a significant rela-tionship with a counselor, a spiritual director, or a life coach. When we cultivate realness in ourselves, our former, apparently simpler lives look very inviting, and many of us choose to return to a surface existence, far removed from the depths of existence we have glimpsed.

Practicing realness inevitably draws upon and awakens our imagination. The Rabbit had to imagine being loved in a way that he had not yet fully experienced in the two hours the Boy had played with him. Martin and Emma imagined themselves being destructive in fantasy so as not to become destructive in reality. Our capacity to imagine shows us a second central aspect of being play-full: practicing creativity.

Practicing Creativity

The creativity of a play-full life is not limited to painting or poetry or pottery or writing and singing or making music or solving riddles or playing Sudoku. When you hold the paradoxical tension inherent to being real, you are practicing creativity. You are creative when you want to criticize but become play-full instead; when you feel lost and confused yet replace that with a certain sense of security; when reactivity would be natural, but you seek ways to be responsive to what is happening. You are creative when you want to remove yourself from a conflict-filled relationship by retreating into silence, but you seek the words to remain present to your partner or friend.

Regardless of how your creativity is present, it invites you to step aside from the burdens of reality, which portrays itself as so undeniably objective. Furthermore, creativity also relieves us of our inner subjectivities that are frighteningly confusing, such as our dream life. Entering into that space between our subjectivity and reality and engaging the intentional fantasy inherent to creativity is life-giving and awakens an adventurous spirit. Creativity invites us into the space between the signs we receive from the media and culture and the symptoms we embody. We do not have an asthma attack when our emotional environment becomes suffocating. We need not get a migraine headache when something is going against our grain. We need not suffer acid reflux when we cannot stomach authority over us or something else. We need not become hungry when we feel emotionally or relationally starved.

We need not become allergic to pets when we want to thumb our nose at others. We need not endure constipation because we find ourselves stuck in situations or in relationships or when we feel we are losing control. A play-full life is an *embodied* life, always seeking meaning in the symptoms our body portrays. In this creative space, filled with potential, we grow beyond the tyranny of fact — "We have lost our jobs" — or the abstract nature of (spiritual) denial — "God will take care of us." This creative space becomes a place where we live.

What symptom does your body offer you? What is the meaning of that symptom?

Being curious about our inner life is a central aspect of practicing creativity. Some people, sadly, are not curious about their inner lives at all! A few years ago I was invited to speak to a church group. I informed them that my topic would be "Living in the Third World." When I entered the building, it was decorated in an African theme. There were masks and spears, carved animals, and beaded jewelry hanging on the walls. The person who extended the invitation to me knew that I was born and raised in South Africa. He thought I was going to talk about what it was like growing up in an Apartheid society since he saw South Africa as a third world country and communicated that to the group. I, however, came prepared to talk about creative living that offers us a "third world" to live in beyond our subjectivity and beyond objectivity. After some initial anxiety on my part, we had a good laugh. I learned to be clearer in my communication when I am invited to address a group. But I also learned that some people would rather hear about other people growing up amidst lions and elephants and in a destructive social system rather than face their own lives and embrace the challenge to live creatively.

SueEllen is an aspiring professional photographer. "I am a great photographer," she states. She has spent months and spends hours each day drafting possible projects for her portfolio, which contain only a few images that meet her own high expectations. She is interested in doing a photo exposé on "the children of musicians," "the trees of Yosemite," and "life through the lens of dementia." SueEllen's father is a successful musician, her favorite family memory is a trip to Yosemite, and her grandmother was diagnosed with Alzheimer's Disease. As she faced her own lack of play-fullness, she recognized that she feels safe in a world where she contemplates ideas for her portfolio. Taking pictures, placing them in a portfolio, and showing it to people awakens a great fear in her. Her anxiety, fueled by a very active inner critic and a competitive spirit to be the best, kept her from actually following through on her ideas and building her portfolio. Wanting to work on three themes, she was advised by her counselor to adopt the "rule of thirds." The "rule" states that one-third of people who look at her work might dismiss it as "bad"; one-third might be indifferent, saying "so what" or "whatever"; and, one-third will appreciate her work and be drawn in by her images. Her counselor stated that as long as the people who love her work are not always the same group of people, she might be a good-enough photographer to become a professional. Finding the courage to show a few galleries her work, she was surprised that she exceeded her adopted "rule of thirds" as many more folks affirmed her work than were indifferent to it or actively disliked it. She even found two galleries interested in showing her work.

What forms of creativity invite you into a "third world?" Engage in those activities more frequently.

SueEllen experienced inner freedom from the rigid defenses her inner critic and perfectionism placed on her. These defenses awakened compulsivity in her, taking her day after day through the same anguish of contemplating ideas and looking at images she inevitably dismissed as "bad." Creativity, however, does not know the thoughtless repetition that comes with compulsivity even if practicing things over and over again makes one a better artist. Rather, she recognized she has an *inner innovator,* a voice, similar to the inner critic, but one that fosters creative living and responsiveness. This voice, however, never volunteers itself, but has to be called out as if it is an elusive animal hiding in a forest. When called, the inner innovator shows itself most often, for God gifts every person with creativity and such a voice. SueEllen also had to face her worst fear: Who will she be if she discovers that some people do indeed consider her a really bad photographer? Entering into our deepest fears is part of becoming emotionally and relationally mature. Growing in play-fullness, SueEllen realized that external forces couldn't purely determine her sense of self. As she dialogued with her inner critic her fear of others rejecting her work diminished.

What "rules" have you created for yourself that help you live creatively? How can the "rule of thirds" speak into your own life?

Play-fullness beckons us to view creativity as much more than knitting, gardening, cooking, reading, painting, doodling, picking up an instrument, or singing, even though all these activities can help you grow in play-fullness. Creative living takes countless shapes:

+ Dreaming in color, and keeping a dream journal

+ Accessing your emotional life

+ Cooking a meal and eating it with loved ones and friends

- Allowing the creativity of others to enrich you, whether in conversation and relationship, in book form, as music, or in museums and other galleries

- Communing with your Creator and celebrating and enjoying the creative acts of God

- Discovering yourself and seeing others in new ways

- Engaging reality with the knowledge that other worlds, such as the subjective world or the world of the imagination, are equally important

- Entering into and engaging nature or culture

- Expressing gratitude

- Imagining a world where peace and justice reigns

- Facing your worst fears

- Finding creativity in that which is not unusual, extraordinary, or relegated to the most gifted or skilled individuals

- Greeting neighbors and other persons

- Growing in your capacity to enter solitude

- Holding others with a lightness of touch

- Improvising and innovating

- Listening to your intuition

- Looking for alternatives

- Nurturing your body

- Praying in silence and with words, with eyes shut and wide open, while stationary or moving

- Receiving freedom in creative activities, such as drawing, woodworking, and knitting

- Recognizing the interwovenness of your mind, body, and spirit

- Relaxing after a busy day, maybe by taking a long bath or shower, or by walking around the block

- Releasing your aggression in ways that cause no harm to others; destroying only in fantasy
- Resisting conformity and other forms of idol worship
- Sensing and emotionally accepting your own brokenness and woundedness
- Trusting creative imagination as life-giving

How do you empower yourself to engage in a few of these creative ways of living?

We often associate creativity with being an artist, which is unfortunate, for God created in all of us an imagination that supports creative living in myriad ways. We need creative imagination to have faith and to be hopeful persons. Like many artists who feel anxious when they stare at a blank canvas or writers when they see an empty screen on their computer or a blank page, creative living is not a life void of anxiety. The tension inherent to creative living, however, is rarely overwhelming and debilitating, but becomes a catalyst for change, growth, and the loving of self and others.

Imagine you are an artist. What would you create?

Creative imagination cannot be reduced to fantasy. Fantasy, as Martin and Emma showed us, can be used as a mature defense against anxieties such as uncertainty and against hurts such as rejection. However, fantasy is also used in the service of boredom, daydreaming, escaping from reality, or entering a virtual reality. These forms of fantasy are often fueled by *frustration*. Frustration awakens anxiety, and activities like daydreaming or losing ourselves in virtual reality releases that tension. Creative living, however, requires much more intentionality than daydreaming requires. As is true of all defenses, using fantasy for tension-release can help us significantly in the short term. However, if a defense mechanism becomes a way of living, often consuming much time at the expense of personal growth and relationships, our play-fullness and quality of life greatly diminishes. Fantasy then supports withdrawal, isolation, and private experiences. Creative living, most often, seeks connection with others. It takes us into community, including a deeper relationship with ourselves. Still, fantasy and the imaginary worlds it creates play an important role in our lives. It invigorates us and offers much needed release, even if only for a short while. Persons who participate in a "virtual" sport league — fantasy football, for example — often experience joy from such activities. Play-fullness, however, is firmly grounded in reality, and fantasy alone is not strong enough to keep us rooted.

Balance your fantasy activities, such as playing video games and daydreaming, with creative activities.

Practicing Boundlessness

God without borders. We are created into that image. Surely, if we have Doctors, Architects, Volunteers, Engineers, Mental Health Workers, Translators, and even Aviators, *all without borders*, then we too can experience a borderless, boundless life. Almost all religious scriptures describe this attribute of boundlessness or spaciousness of God. The prophet Elisha, who fed the enemies others wanted to kill, gives us a glimpse of the boundlessness, or flowing nature, of God. A man associated with Elisha died. His widow became bitter, asking: Why God? Why did he have to die? Why am I on the brink of financial ruin? Who is going to care for me? About to lose her two children to a creditor, she visits with Elisha, half-blaming him and his God. Elisha asks her what she possesses that has any value. She answers that she has only a small jar of olive oil, used for cooking and for medicinal purposes. Elisha tells her to collect as many empty vessels as possible, and then behind closed doors pour her little bit of oil into the jars. She follows the prophet's orders, and soon all the jars she can lay her hands on are filled. She returns to Elisha, who advises her to sell the oil to her neighbors, use some of the money to pay off her debt, and use the leftover oil for personal use. Soon the blessings the widow received flow into her neighborhood. The jars of oil were filled, but so too the life of this widow, whose mourning took on new meaning: the lives of her children, who received a new future other than being slaves, and the lives of her neighbors, who could cook and treat ailments with the oil. The blessing that flowed from God flowed to many unnamed persons in an unnamed town. Previously hamstrung by grief and resentment, the widow experiences boundless grace.

This age-old story has modern versions. Milton Erickson was a prominent psychiatrist who taught at a medical school. Struck with polio in childhood, Erickson lived a boundless life even though he spent most of it in a wheelchair. Though unable to walk, he undertook a thousand mile canoe trip, discovering his body could do things he never thought possible. As Elisha's widow passed on her freedom to others, so too did Erickson. One day a student in one of Erickson's classes became concerned about an aunt whose emotional state placed her life in danger. The student asked whether Erickson could see her, and the next day Erickson made a home visit. Upon entering her home, he asked the woman if she would show him her house. The woman lived a cloistered life in a somewhat unkempt house. Going through the house, Erickson saw a sun porch with rows of African violets, and being a doctor, Erickson gave the woman a prescription: he told her to look at the local newspaper's announcements of births, significant birthdays, weddings, and deaths. She should then send the individual or family an African violet with a note saying that it is from her. Erickson never heard from the woman again. Twenty years passed and a newspaper article announced: "The African Violet Queen Dies at Age 76." The article recalled how significant a person she was to her church and community. For this woman, growing African violets and giving gifts to others formed the cornerstones of a boundless life. Here too the freedom and blessing found by one woman became a blessing to others.

How do you flow, in life-affirming ways,
to others or to your community?

From the moment we are born we anticipate our deaths. Limits are inherent to life, yet one can experience life as flowing, abundant, inexhaustible, endless, unfailing, infinite, ceaseless, and everlasting despite those limits. Play-fullness is boundless and beckons you to move beyond a life constrained by boundaries and limits, beyond a life that knows only winners and losers. *A life that reverberates with vitality and energy is possible.* This life may remain elusive if life-giving and life-affirming energy rarely flows, first to you and then from you to enrich and nurture others. Boundlessness invites you to discover something new about yourself, others, God, nature, and life in general. Certainly we can live a life that is confined by time, measured by numbers, limited by space, governed by rules, or controlled by relationships. But what a sad life this would be! It is *within* the presence of time and numbers and relationships that you discover boundlessness. Whether it is resisting selling your soul to an idol such as materialism; whether it is setting aside a day on which your soul rests; whether you commit to nonviolence; whether you deny yourself the thrill of an irresponsible relationship with a person or an image; or whether you contain the urge to pinch or plagiarize — in whatever way you do it, living with boundaries is life-giving and assures healthy lives, relationships, and communities. Boundlessness does not suggest anarchy or a sense of general lawlessness. Rather, boundlessness recognizes the importance of boundaries knowing that a life without boundaries is at risk of becoming tragic. However, a play-full life also knows that boundaries rarely only confine and restrict but instead ultimately give structure and purpose.

A boundless life has *purpose;* sometimes it is found in filling and selling jars with oil and other times in growing African violets and sending them to others. But let's not confuse having purpose with being driven. A life of purpose is passionate, rarely driven. As we saw in chapter 1, drivenness is about internal anxieties and the corruption of play-fullness into a compulsion. Drivenness is maintained only at significant cost and then only for short periods of time. Sadly, many of us live in a world that believes that spiritual purposes are more important than more earthy ones. Such a view is unfortunate, for God wants us to thrive in the ordinary walks of our lives! Planting and tending African violets to give away provide all the purpose one needs to live as a queen or king.

What activities do you engage in that remind you of the abundance of life?

Time: we either have too little, which happens most often, or we seem to have too much. *Have you noticed the odd language we use to describe our relationship with time?* We say: "I must be on time," "I have no time," or, "I'm just killing time," or "I'm making time." Sometimes we say: "Time is money" or "I need to buy time." Many of us feel as if we are "on the clock." Sociologists tell us that we talk about time in the same manner hungry people talk about food! In a world where time is in short demand, time is a commodity that remains elusive. We seem so rushed: always wanting things to happen right here, right now! We may have more ways to talk about time than ways to describe a balanced, meaningful life! How do you experience time? Where do you experience freedom from time or have time to spare?

Take note of the language you use to describe your relationship with time.

The experience of time is *an emotional experience,* similar to our experience of money. If we feel rushed — emotionally, spiritually, relationally, or even economically — time is in short supply. *Remember how slowly time passed when you were bored as a kid?* "Are we there yet?" you would ask your mom or dad repeatedly while driving on vacations as your inner world slowed down, deprived of the usual stimulations. If you are in a balanced place, however, possibly losing yourself in a good novel, time is suspended and a few hours feel like minutes.

Engage in an activity that suspends your experience of time but does not involve electronic equipment such as a television, a computer, a phone, or a video game.

We also recognize the boundless nature of play-fullness in the following:

- Viewing life in terms of participation, not as winning or losing
- Having relationships *with* people guards against turning people into things or matter or titles
- Preferring strength over power
- Considering thoughts as more important than knowledge

- Keeping boundaries that do not stifle, but always have room for play-fullness

- Determining health by the presence of relationship and meaning and not by the absence of disease

- Never excluding play-fullness with seriousness

- Remembering that processes are vital, while predicting outcomes is defensive

- Knowing that authentic speech creates intimacy, whereas using the voice and words of others rather than your own causes distance and hides deeper insecurities

- Constantly reinterpreting oneself in light of present experiences and future expectations

- Knowing that life is a gift to give away, only to receive it back

- Resisting the genitalization of sexuality that focuses on specific body parts only

- Communing with nature rather than idealizing, demonizing, or controlling it

- Longing for aliveness in death and avoiding being dead in life

> The next time you play *Monopoly,* deliberately lose all your money and identify with a third of all people on earth living on less than $2 a day.

Boundlessness inevitably takes one into *nature,* where you discover a relationship *with* nature. As you seek a life beyond ownership, consumption, and control, you produce less waste and so protect the earth's limited resources. As you listen to weather forecasts, for example, you have no doubt noticed that we have a highly ambivalent relationship with nature, a relationship we tend to either idealize or demonize. You have probably heard of "perfect" or "severe" weather, a "killer" or "monster" storm, "extreme" heat, and "ferocious" winds. You might be summoned to become a "weather warrior" or discover that you are indifferent to nature. We live climate-controlled lives and are seventy-degree persons.

Maybe we can learn from Aboriginal Australians, who traditionally have a significant relationship with their environment. On the vast expanses of the Australian Outback, a land that calls forth boundless living, Aboriginal Australians have a beautiful word to describe a way of life that is in harmony with nature: *dadirri*. The word describes being at peace with oneself, with your Creator, and with nature. *Dadirri* recognizes the sacredness of nature and hears the invitation to follow her rhythms. It is to walk in contemplation and in balance with the seasons, trusting that whether it is spring, summer, fall, or winter, nature sustains life. If we listen to nature, nature becomes a known mystery.

Spend some time listening to nature.
Rediscover nature as the giver of life
and as your home.

The boundless nature of play-fullness is beautifully portrayed in the difference between approaching life as a *tourist* or as a *traveler*. A tourist, for example, often *overcomes* vast distances at great speeds and eagerly asks: "Are we there yet?" Travelers, on the other hand, *discover* distance, recognizing there are many ways to travel from point A to point B and that the journey between destinations itself might be the "vacation." Tourists tend to *look at* things and therefore see much; travelers have new experiences, often *with* people and new environs. The differences between being a tourist and being a traveler in life are many and significant.

Tourist	Traveler
Being on time with a fixed schedule (*Chronos*)	Experiencing the moment, possibly a sunset or sunrise (*Kairos*)
Looking at people or animals	*Communing with* people or nature
Preferring *individuality* and to be left alone	Seeking *the company of others*
Arriving at Point B	Appreciating the *journey*
Taking *risks* and seeking sensation	*Discerning* with mindfulness and care
Paying for a *problem-free* trip; no adversity	*Expecting problems* to be solved; some adversity
Showing *disinterest*	*Growing* in cultural awareness
Expecting hospitality and great lodging	*Receiving hospitality* as a gift, whatever lodging is provided
Exchanging *money*	Exchanging *lives*
Indulging behavior	*Giving up* privileges
Doing things, constantly	*Being* relaxed
Wanting "all inclusive" locations	*Seeking* the road less traveled
Changing of skin color and girth (due to sun and food)	*Transformation* of heart and soul (due to being touched by someone else's life)
Religion without being religious	*Religious* with or without having religion

Boundlessness, as you've recognized, does not require exotic vacations or other experiences. By taking a different path back to your home, for example, or by seeking out bird and animal life along the way, you can experience boundlessness even in your immediate area, just a few miles from home. So too can a travel magazine or television program transport you to foreign places and into the lives of strangers. Finding a pen pal or learning a foreign language through peer teaching will increase your boundlessness.

Boundlessness also addresses our sense of spirituality. A play-full life is a spiritual, religious life, even if one may not have a strong relationship with religion. Religion without a deeper spiritual core is seen in the person praying in church or on street corners to be seen by others, or in the person who judges others according to preconceived beliefs and stereotypes. Boundless spirituality, on the other hand, is seen in the person who prays not to be seen by others, but who converses with the unseen God. It is the person who wants to feed when others want to kill, whether by words or, worse, through violence.

How would your world change if you were to approach it with the attitude of being a traveler in life?

For the person with religion but without play-full boundlessness, the stories of faith have to be *explained,* for they have meaning that *must* be given and demand *obedience and submission.* There is thus much talking and in the process the stories lose their mythic nature. In a play-full spirituality, the stories of faith remain a mystery worthy of *retelling* or *reenacting,* for the stories give meaning that might be discovered as a gift. In boundless living there is much listening and discernment, with a significant amount of resonance and acceptance. As the stories are retold or reenacted, they receive sacred, life-giving qualities that invite *surrendering* and *participation*. You say: "I believe, . . . " even as one recognizes that the statement you make is incomplete. It recognizes that the Sabbath is for rest, not for church programs or shopping. Someone said that a person lacking boundlessness worships in shopping malls that come and go, while a boundless person worships in cathedrals that offer a spiritual home to many generations. Sadly, the way we do church, synagogue, or religious life most often diminishes boundless play-fullness. Play-fullness resists such a depiction and seeks the freedom one finds in a life lived to the full. It finds God at play, not only in creation, but also in moments of life, death, and resurrection.

> What daily spiritual practices do you engage in?

A boundless, play-full life experiences life as flowing, abundant, inexhaustible, endless, unfailing, infinite, ceaseless, and everlasting. Without much effort, our lives become stuck, deficient, inadequate, finite, marginal, and faltering. The latter mind-set soon takes us to a competitive world of opponents, enemies, and winners and losers, a world where exploitation and the fittest rule. A boundless life does not create or celebrate winners and losers, for it recognizes that if one suffers, all suffer. It thus seeks the well-being of everyone, even persons who remain nameless and faceless in far corners of the world, in some forsaken prisons, or persons whose lives (and lifestyles) we do not fully understand. Boundlessness invites us to find freedom within and without, discovering possibility and opportunity as it receives the gifts of love, joy, peace, patience, gentleness, goodness, faithfulness, kindness, and self-control.

In Conclusion

The cartoon stated: "We want you to be more creative . . . more imaginative in your work . . . and this is how we want you to do it!" It showed a man behind a desk being handed a pile of papers, at least a yard high. The face of the man receiving the paper stack just dropped, obviously not feeling creative or imaginative at that moment. Practicing realness, creativity, and boundlessness are three core traits of a play-full life. This life is neither hard work nor is it time-consuming, but it is intentional work, requiring mindfulness and commitment. The reward is an inner peace and sense of freedom that far surpasses anything a world driven by *criticism, control, compulsion,* and the other enemies of play can provide.

Next, we look at three related play-full practices: Slowness, Hospitality, and Transcendence.

THREE

Play-fullness Practicing (Part 2)
Slowness, Hospitality, and Transcendence

Realness, discussed in the previous chapter, challenges you to hold paradox and resist dichotomous thinking. *Creativity* invites you to use and nurture your imagination. *Boundlessness*, in turn, beckons you to move beyond a life constrained by boundaries where only winners and losers reside. As the title suggests, this chapter discusses three additional play-full practices: *slowness, hospitality, and transcendence:*

- *Slowness* encourages you to do things at the right speed, to savor the tastes, smells, sights, and sounds of life, to touch life gently and not to rush through time and space.

- *Hospitality* calls on you to create space for yourself and others where you and they can grow.

- *Transcendence* summons you to experience awe and wonder.

I imagine that the way you envision your life is changing in exciting ways. So too is your life and relationships colored by peace and a sense of general well-being as positive, life-giving energy flows within you and between you and others. Practicing slowness, hospitality, and transcendence is going to have a similar influence on your life.

Practicing Slowness

One answer to the question: *What did Jesus do?* is, he walked. Being a peasant, Jesus rarely had the luxury of riding horses or even donkeys. He lived a slow life. *A play-full life is lived at the right speed.* It is to have *enough time* to live with joy and in community with others. Slowness encourages you to slow down, to savor the relationships, tastes, smells, sights, and sounds of life; to touch life gently. Slowing down in a world that is racing ahead is a challenge, but so freeing! Images of slowness and being rushed, especially the latter, abound. God's people walked for forty years in a desert. God's warrior Joshua asked God to stop the sun and the moon and it happened. The road Jesus took to being crucified, the way of the cross, was a slow road. Much later Simon and Garfunkel sang: "Slow down, you move too fast, you've got to make the morning last. . . . " Working in New York a few years ago I would see people literally running toward Pennsylvania Station at day's end to catch a crowded commuter train, otherwise risking an hour's wait for the next train. Often I would join the runners. "Slow down, you move too fast. . . . "

Most of us live *The Fast Life.* Everything has to be faster and needs to happen zippity quick. Author Carl Honoré calls it the *velocitization* of life. We want our red lights to be green; our morning commute to be congestion free so that we can speed along at seventy plus miles an hour; our air travel to be on time. We want to be able to drive up and buy what we need. We want overnight shipping of our online purchases, and we seek fast processors for our computers and fast Internet access. We want many channels to surf on television; recorded television shows without advertisement breaks; constant alerts from our Smartphone; our phone directory on speed dial; our e-mails to be answered immediately; the stock exchange to rebound quickly; our weight loss program to show great results in seven days or less; and, of course, we want fast food. In the United States we have become a "Fast Food Nation" and we are exporting this lifestyle around the world at frightening speeds. Because we experience life as a race, our relationships, including our relationship with nature, and our souls become strained and depleted as our need for speed, control, and instant gratification increases. Our bodies become stressed. The

Fast Life is a rushed life — an unsustainable life. Far from being cheap, this life comes at great cost.

> How do you participate in "The Fast Life?"

It seems as if we all have a deep need to slow things down, especially if we find ourselves in the chaos of war, as was the case for Joshua, or in the frenzy of a fast-paced life, running half-crazy between work and home and family responsibilities. The need to slow things down exposes an even deeper need: *the need to live in balance.* Practicing slowness as an integral part of play-fullness describes not only our relationship with time, but also our relationships with ourselves, others, and nature. It envisions lives and relationships that are lovingly nurtured and sustained. If we have an emotional relationship with time, packing more into every hour is not necessarily a recipe for healthy living. Honoré writes that we are victims of the *cult of speed,* a cult that gives us the illusion that to survive we need to speed up! Twice I had to ask the publisher to delay the publication date of this book because I had been unrealistic about the pace of writing a book that is more about inviting and sharing than writing. I could not write this book *zippity quick!* Like a slow cooked meal, prepared with care and in the presence of friends, *A Play-full Life* as a book took form within me and on my computer while in conversation with others and myself.

> What would slowing down look like for you? Name any fears, anxieties, and expectations that come to you as you imagine a slower paced life.

Practicing slowness has its roots in the Slow Food Movement and describes *a way of living.* It started in 1986 when Italian Carlos Petrini and others protested the building of a McDonald's restaurant on the plaza at the Spanish Steps in the center of Rome. With a bowl of pasta, Petrini and his friends stood against the global standardization of food and especially the primary values undergirding fast food and the fast life: production, efficiency, speed, and profit. In 1989, representatives from fifteen countries gathered in Paris and pledged to preserve the diversity of the world's food and culinary practices by teaching people about food production and supply. The countercultural Slow Food Movement — which has no central headquarters or representative — reminds us that cooking a meal at home with locally grown ingredients, practicing eco-gastronomy, and the ritual of eating together can feed our imaginations, awaken our senses, and transform our relationships to be more compassionate, communal, and convivial. Petrini reminded the world of how important it is to cook ordinary food using fresh produce from local farmers to be eaten around the family table while enjoying a glass of wine or juice. It is the celebration of a different way of living. The Slow Food Movement began as an Italian protest against powerful economic forces and is now a presence in more than a hundred countries where local small farms and indigenous products are cultivated, protected, and brought into a sustainable market economy.

Begin your practice of slowness by eating foods that are locally produced. Think of joining a farming co-op, or, better yet, plant your own vegetable garden.

In addition to the practices of slowness already mentioned, deepen your play-fullness by:

- Resting one day of the week — keeping Sabbath
- Walking a labyrinth
- Watching less television
- Walking or bicycling as much as you can
- Listening to what your body tells you
- Experiencing the moment, paying attention, and practicing mindfulness
- Going to bed at a regular time assuring you at least eight hours of sleep
- Letting your natural rhythms awaken you
- Turning off your cell phone
- Lighting candles
- Buying fair trade products
- Visiting a farmers' market
- Using a slow-cooker
- Eating with people
- Baking bread
- Brewing beer
- Making your own wine
- Chewing your food well before swallowing
- Keeping a food journal
- Sitting on a porch
- Helping children run a lemonade stand
- Washing dishes by hand
- Air drying (or sun drying) washed clothing
- Brushing your teeth for two minutes
- Purchasing recycled clothing
- Hiking a section of a trail

- ◆ Growing bonsai trees
- ◆ Spending a day at a museum
- ◆ Using a manual push mower
- ◆ Deepening a few significant friendships
- ◆ Sitting down during a conversation
- ◆ Meeting with someone or calling someone
- ◆ Leaving a few minutes earlier for appointments
- ◆ Using cash and not a credit card
- ◆ Traveling by train or boat
- ◆ Staying in bed when sick
- ◆ Aging with intentionality

Slow Living is not about doing everything at a snail's pace, even though the snail is the symbol of the Slow Food Movement. It is about working, playing, and living better by doing everything at the right speed; about being mindful that our natural resources are limited and that forces of consumerism and homogenization turn persons into products. By being slow, you recognize that your quality of life depends on how you spend your time. It thus describes a way of living that embodies specific values — one value being that the preparation of food and eating together brings flavor to your life.

> Resist buying any fast food for a week,
> including take-out coffee or tea.

Other values include the recognition of the rhythm of nature's offerings; the recognition that pleasure is not the same as hedonism; that creative living engages tradition and is responsible for the future; and that slowness needs to be practiced. Slowness bespeaks breathing and being calm, being patient, mindful, responsive, receptive, unhurried, choosing quality over quantity. Fast Living, in turn, bespeaks hyperventilation, busyness, and being impatient, reactive, hurried, seeking quantity over quality.

Prepare a meal using ingredients produced within a hundred miles or less of your home. Share the meal with friends.

The Stoddart family joined a local CSA (Community Supported Agriculture) group in which two twenty-something college-educated women engage in organic farming. In a CSA, one purchases stock in a farm, which then provides you with fresh fruit and vegetables. Suddenly the family's life is transformed. Before the harvest even began to come in, the family visited the farm where the children learned about organic farming principles and worked for a few hours with the farmers. Heavy rains brought out snails that threatened the tomato crop. After a barn raising-like call to all the shareholders, the family handpicked the snails off the tomato plants with many other families. Early squeamishness about touching snails soon was replaced by laughter as the family thought of recipes in which they could use the snails. Their favorites were "snailut butter," which they envisioned could be used to make jelly sandwiches, and "snesto," a pesto-like product. Once a week the family goes to a central collection spot where they receive produce that was harvested a few hours earlier. Receiving vegetables they never ate before such as arugula, bok choi, collards, kale, kohlrabi, leeks, and tat soi, the family researched different recipes, some to eat immediately and some to preserve the vegetables and fruit for later use. Most weeks the family received enough vegetables to share with friends. The family was surprised to discover that the fruit and vegetables they received from the farm lasted much longer than store-bought produce. The children measured their carbon footprint and were proud to see it shrinking.

Practicing slowness simplifies all aspects of life: loving, working, relationships, and various forms of consuming. The Slow Food Movement follows "The Noah Principle," arguing that everything has been done to master the world, cultures, traditions, and the ecosystem, and all are now in need of *salvation*. As Noah's ark protected its passengers, so too do we need to create sanctuaries that protect. And since Noah brought onboard the ark only healthy food and clean water, so too do we need to be mindful about the food we consume and the water we protect. Practicing slowness encourages sustainable, organic practices and resists the genetic modification of foodstuffs. It resists giving growth hormones to cows, for example, so that they deliver more milk. Not only do we drink that milk, but also when the cows inevitably end up in fast food meats, we eat high levels of unnatural hormones.

Identify five distinct tastes in your next meal.

Preparing home-cooked meals that are eaten in conversation with others is an important part of practicing slowness. It is, of course, closely related to practicing hospitality, another key aspect of play-fullness. We all know that as families we tend to eat less and less together, and when we do eat together, our conversations remain superficial, sharing facts and data with each other, rather than sharing our emotional or relational or spiritual lives. Imagine coming home from work, for example, and instead of letting your body language tell your family that you've had a crummy day, or instead of telling about this or that happening at work or revisiting that bad driver who nearly ran you off the road, you tell your family what your current emotional state is. If it is frustration or anger or feeling low on energy, own responsibility for your frustration or anger so that your loved ones need not become confused in their relationship with you and try to fix you as if you are a problem. Imagine coming home and telling of the joy or peace you feel, for on the way home you saw a beautiful cloud formation that reminded you of God. Telling someone that you love him or her in such a manner that the other person receives your love is a great way to practice slowness. Practices such as prayer, meditation, yoga, *Tai Chi*, and even physical exercise can help you be more present in the moment.

> How do you share less juicy bits of information but more of your affective, relational, or spiritual world with those closest to you today?

As a way of living, practicing slowness fosters peacefulness, calmness, care and compassion, and meditation. It is mindful of the largeness of life, even if forces like capitalism and globalization shrink our reality. Slowness is not against technology or even progress, but it is against the idolization of those forces in our lives that erode well-being. It is also not against speed per se. Who wants to walk cross-country to go on vacation when you can fly from coast to coast? Or who wants to send surface mail letters to replace email communication? It is the *obsession* with speed — indicating compulsion but also consumption — and the destructive ways we attempt to "buy time" that is the concern. Riding cross-country following old Route 66 is a vacation in itself, even as flying from Chicago to Santa Monica on the West Coast takes you to beautiful beaches where you can relax with a good novel.

On the road of life there are many roads like Route 66 worth riding at the right speed, which inevitably implies taking back roads and not interstates. A few years ago I was traveling by motorcycle to an academic conference in Atlanta. I gave myself four days to cover the thousand or so miles. In Indiana the Amish community challenged my metal horse and me to ponder the difference between the twelve hundred horses under my butt and the one horsepower buggies making their way on the side of the road. It was in a valley in West Virginia that I received a gift that remains with me in visceral ways. It was a gift of shelter.

As I followed a meandering road along a narrow valley, a thunderstorm greeted me before I could throw on my rain suit. Seasoned riders know better. With grape-sized raindrops playing deafening drums on my helmet, I recognized that the road had become unsafe. Seeking shelter, I stopped at a dilapidated gas stop, now a store selling antiques. I parked my motorcycle and walked in, soaking wet. It was then that I met Arnold. Unfazed with me being a walking reservoir, he first invited me in only to send me back out in the rain while he opened a garage door so that my motorcycle can "get out of the rain." Realizing that resistance was futile I added more water to my soaked body.

Commit fifteen minutes every day
to meditating on living life at the
right pace.

As I parked my motorcycle in the garage, Arnold shoved a soda into my hand and pulled up two chairs he placed in the doorway. He started off by saying, "I'm a motorcyclist too. . . . There she is, a Harley. . . . She's almost thirty-five years old. . . . I bought her used after I got back from Vietnam." In the corner of the garage stood a dust covered metallic blue motorcycle with American and Prisoner of War flags on the back. The lightning danced as we sat and enjoyed our sodas. Arnold told me that he is retired and that he opened the antique store after "a few failed marriages." Life has been good to him, he continued. "The best part," he said, "is meeting people like you." Hearing my accent, he asked where I came from. We talked about life, war, and religion, and how those forces often come together. Somewhere not too far from here, I thought, are people in cars racing the rain, with wipers working overtime to clear the heavenly grapes that refuse to subside. I'd rather be wet and meet a person like Arnold. Practicing slowness is about living a balanced, "local" life, rooted in place and relationships with self, with others, and with God. This life is not measured in moments or hours or days or weeks. Every moment carries potential to become a play-full one, even if we cannot live into every moment in a play-full manner. Nor does a play-full life end with our own death, but the seeds we planted in others will continue to enrich future generations even as we continue a life beyond the grave.

How do other people notice that you are walking in balance?

Practicing slowness is also a practice of "politics," but maybe not in the way you imagine. "Politics" literally means "the shape of the city." We are always political, always shaping cities. We either shape our lives and the lives of others unconsciously according to principles such as the enemies of play-fullness, or we shape our cities, our families, our relationships, and our lives according to values that are more life-giving and life-affirming. We can learn from the Tohono O'odham Nation of Arizona and Northwest Mexico. They have a beautiful word: *himdag*. (It's a bit like the word *dadirri* that we met earlier.) The word is best translated as "walking in balance." For the Tohono O'odham Nation, *himdag* speaks to the individual and the communal and the spiritual and the relationship between a person and the larger group and the Creator. *Himdag* calls forth respect for self and others, including nature, building strong family relationships, engaging in cultural activities such as storytelling and crafts, and seeking ways to promote emotional, relational, spiritual, and even physical well-being. An individual, family, and community shaped according to the principles of *himdag* practices slowness. Living with *himdag* awakens hospitality.

Practicing Hospitality

Hospitality beckons you to create a space in your home where you and others can grow, for such spaces carry potential. It is extending a welcome to yourself and to others. This act of creating space and extending welcome is a powerful and potential place where three become one. This weird mathematics happened to patriarch Abraham and his wife, Sarah. The elderly couple was camping near the great trees of Mamre when three individuals appeared on the horizon. With his hospitable heart, Abraham invited the three visitors to stay with them for a while, to have their feet washed — an act of hospitality itself — and to drink water and feast with him and Sarah. Abraham asked Sarah to bake fresh bread while he prepared some meat for the meal. It is at this point in the story that the three visitors became One. The Lord, the story continues, informed Abraham that Sarah would give birth to a son within a year's time. Sarah overheard the Lord saying this, and knowing she was past childbearing age, she laughed. The Lord confronted Sarah about her laughing, but she could not admit that she had laughed. A year later Isaac was born.

What an amazing story! The hospitality extended by Abraham not only proved that one could entertain angels unaware, as the Apostle Paul believed too; it also proved that one could entertain even God! Jesus, of course, repeats this truth about hospitality when he tells a parable of a king who separated sheep and goats. The sheep gave food to the hungry and water to the king and they invited the king into their homes and gave him clothes to wear. They also visited him in prison. In short, the sheep lived a life of peace and justice. Strangely, the sheep could not recall the hospitality the king ascribed to them. If one is hospitable and kind to strangers, one is so toward the king.

To be hospitable, especially to strangers, is a spiritual and ethical mandate. God requires it of us. God also required hospitality of the people of Israel, for they were strangers in Egypt, and since they knew what oppression was, they were not to oppress strangers. The mistreatment of those who are "strange" is an act of injustice. Today, strangers are plentiful: some speak Spanish; some walk around wearing black make-up and black clothes with dangling chains; some have a different sexual orientation or an illness such as HIV/AIDS; some are jobless; and some are old and isolated. Repeatedly God's people hear that they should not mistreat strangers. When Job defended himself against his friends, he stated: "I took up the case of the stranger . . . my door was always open to the traveler. . . ." If the language of Israel was caring for the stranger, the language of Jesus' time was that of hospitality. "Practice hospitality" is the succinct challenge the apostle Paul gives to the church in Rome.

> Who will you become if the life-giving
> power of hospitality touches your life?

To be a host to strangers, including friends who you think you know well, is a core trait of a play-full life. Hospitality, however, is not an easy practice to engage in. Our families and cultures have instilled in most of us a deep distrust toward strangers, especially strangers with dark skins if you are white or vice versa if you are a person of color. We distrust people who do not look like us, think like us, act like us, and who do not have a similar bank account or education. Likewise, we are protective of the spaces we call home. Inviting people into our homes makes us anxious, and soon we find reasons why offering hospitality is not possible. *Hospes* (meaning "guest") easily becomes *hostis*, the Latin word for "enemy" or "stranger." *Hostis* gave us our word "hostility," reminding us that the line between a stranger and hostility is a thin one. Following the Lord who visited Abraham and Sarah, and listening to Jesus telling about a king who rewards hospitality, being hospitable is a sign of spiritual, emotional, and relational maturity.

Recall one experience where hospitality turned a stranger into a friend.

A hospitable space is a place where the contradictions of life such as joy and sadness are honored. Christine's husband of nearly forty years, Rick, died unexpectedly just as the couple envisioned early retirement and traveling to all the places in the world they always wanted to see. Married shortly after they finished high school, Christine became a mother and homemaker, more by fate than by choice. With Rick working for a government agency that often took him on the road, Christine did most of the parenting of their three children. Rick's death catapulted Christine into sadness so deep some might consider it a depression. She rarely left the house, and despite her children's encouragement to come and visit with them, Christine remained isolated.

It was after Rick's death that their good friends Deb and Bob started to invite Christine over for dinner. They had known Christine and Rick for years. Rick was Bob's hunting partner, and Christine and Deb raised their children together. The invitation soon became a Wednesday night ritual. At first, Deb and Bob would prepare special meals, but soon they recognized that the time together was more important than any preparations, and so they decided to offer Christine whatever they would have eaten that night. Often they would think of what to prepare only after Christine knocked on their door. Initially, their conversations often turned to Rick. Tears would flow, angry words would be spoken about the unfairness of his untimely death, and happy moments were recalled. Bob shared how on a hunting trip a few years back, Rick got his pants caught on the tree stand he was getting into, only to rip his pants from top to bottom. He fixed them with duct tape but was so flustered that he lost his aim for the rest of the weekend. They all laughed.

Deb and Bob became witnesses as Christine searched for a new identity. Little in life had prepared Christine to be almost sixty, single, and grieving. Like a teenager who discovers her identity in challenging her parents, Christine became defiant. Deb and Bob listened gracefully as Christine would ask for advice only to reject their opinions. As the months progressed, Christine showed greater independence and even canceled a Wednesday night or two because she had agreed to another commitment. Her sadness lifted, and a side of Christine appeared that Deb and Bob had not known: she decided to self-publish a novel and now spends a few hours every morning with her laptop.

The whole process since Rick's death was not always easy for Deb and Bob, and sometimes they felt helpless as they witnessed Christine's sadness, yearning, and searching. They knew, however, that their task was to be hosts and not counselors or advice-givers. Intuitively they recognized that a host and hostess makes room for his or her guests. They discovered that, as they listened to the ways Christine verbalized her loss and searched for a new identity, their appreciation for each other as intimate partners deepened. They started talking more often and about more significant things, such as how they envision their aging process and whether one would consider marrying again should the other die. They encouraged each other to follow their individual dreams. Bob started building a miniature railroad, while Deb invited a friend to travel with her to a spa where for four days, they would be manicured and pampered. Being hosts improved their marriage, but also prompted them to follow personal hobbies and interests.

Practicing slowness anticipates practicing hospitality. Since preparing home-cooked meals shared by friends and family around a table is integral to practicing slowness, hospitality follows almost naturally.

Who might you invite to enjoy a home-cooked meal with you? What food can you prepare only after the guest or guests have arrived as you all move into the kitchen?

We avoid hospitality for many seemingly good reasons. *Criticism* keeps us from becoming hospitable. If your inner voice tells you that you are not a good cook or that your house is in disarray, the likelihood that you will invite friends or even soon-to-be friends for a meal diminishes greatly. So too when *control* has corrupted our sense of play-fullness, for control may not allow us to risk the freedom a guest inevitably embodies. What would happen if your guest acted offensively or says something you do not agree with? Or what if they do not like your food despite your asking about their food preferences? *Compulsion* also inhibits your hospitable nature. If you have certain rituals related to eating, for example, having people over for dinner can be a threat to those established patterns. What do you pray when you invite your Muslim friends for dinner? All the enemies of play-fullness prohibit your hospitable spirit. Furthermore, you may defend yourself against hospitality, for you are uncomfortable being a guest in someone else's house. You know that if you extend an invitation, one might be returned to you. Being a guest requires us to be open to receiving, to being treated as if we were special. For many people, such treatment is uncomfortable, and they'd rather be a host.

Being hospitable to others almost always begins with being hospitable to yourself. Having a relationship with your past without falling into shame or forgetful amnesia is but one way you are hospitable to yourself. Likewise, if you cannot be welcoming to your own strangeness and to the enemies of play-fullness in your life, being hospitable to others may elude you. To practice hospitality, therefore, invites you to befriend yourself, even those emotions, like desire or sadness, that become so unwieldy and overwhelming as they surprise you yet again. It asks you to give shelter and nurturance to the body you dislike, be it apple or pear-shaped, for neither shape conforms to the messages about body-image you received from your parents or the media. As a friend pointed out to me, hospitality requires you to recognize that the margins of your life are someone else's center, and what you see as the center of your life is someone else's margin.

> How do you welcome your own imperfections, your body that you dislike, or your past with its secrets and skeletons?

In the root of *hospitality* one also finds the Latin word *hostire*, which means "to equalize." Inviting someone for a meal literally lets us see eye-to-eye; it brings equality between host and guest; it builds community and fosters a sense of mutuality and belonging. The ancient Greeks believed one had to invite a stranger into one's home, wash the person's feet, offer wine and food, and only then could one ask the person's name. Jared, who offered me hospitality in Albuquerque when my motorcycle malfunctioned on the mountain, followed this age-old custom.

> What reasons do you offer yourself for not being more hospitable? How are the enemies of play-fullness influencing your reasons?

A number of years ago we moved to our current town when I accepted an invitation to teach there. After a couple of years, I was still finding it difficult to make male friends outside my workplace. I had many acquaintances but few friends, and my basic need for male intimacy remained unmet. Wanting to be responsive to my own needs, I started a M.E.A.T. *Club:* Men Eating Animals Together. The idea of a M.E.A.T. *Club* was introduced to me during my doctoral studies. It is not really a club as much as it is a closed group. I invited a person I did not know well and who has a different approach to life to be co-chair of the group with me. Together we invited six more men with different interests and occupations. We eat together every six to eight weeks and rotate from one home to another. The only "bylaws" of our club are that we have a price limit for the cost of each meal and spouses and family members are not allowed to help in the preparation of the food. So inevitably we grill a lot, for men do that. And we eat bread and tossed salads. The real feast, however, is the company and conversation. We laugh and joke, always talk about religion and politics and the economy, and share vulnerabilities and empathy as we and our families experience the roller coaster of life. Through the son of one member, our M.E.A.T. *Club* spun off another chapter in New York City. They too are thriving. We are certainly aware that having "Eating" and "Animals" in relationship will offend some, for not everyone eats meat. Finding other "A-words" proved no challenge, but we decided that eating "apples" might get stale; eating "abalone" is expensive; adding "agave" did not sweeten the deal; "alcohol" would put us at risk; having "appetizers" may not still our hunger; and, eating "alpacas" takes us back to meat. Finding another word for animals, of course, will not change the acronym. . . . Ultimately, the M.E.A.T *Club* is not about animals or meat, but about offering hospitality, being a guest in someone else's home, and discovering each other over a shared meal. One finds all kinds of groups in our society, whether a quilting group, a book group, or a wine club. Why not start a dining group?

Hospitality is much more than being hospitable to oneself or having people over for a meal. Practicing hospitality is the result of an adventurous self. Grow in being hospitable by:

- Accepting your past
- Smiling often
- Looking people in the eye
- Sharing your life, not only your space
- Being compassionate
- Carrying or lightening someone's burdens
- Praying with and for someone
- Extending grace to someone
- Being an advocate for the marginalized and the voiceless; changing oppressive social structures
- Visiting a homebound person, someone in the hospital, or someone in prison
- Refraining from gossip or spreading negative rumors; keeping confidences
- Not letting someone consume alcohol and drive
- Expressing gratitude
- Watching the drama *Babette's Feast* (1988; directed by Gabriel Axel)

A play-full person practices hospitality. Having people over for a meal — whether it is the neighborhood kids who are playing with your children when hunger overwhelms them, or a spontaneous meal with friends, or even a planned dinner with the family who recently moved into your neighborhood — will enrich your life. It creates space where you partake in peace and allow a sense of justice to reign inside you but also between you and others. Hospitality gives you the opportunity to be there for others, just as God has been there for you.

Practicing Transcendence

Think of a time when you have been moved. Not in a physical way,
but in a deeply spiritual and emotional way, and possibly in rela-
tion to someone or something else. I'm thinking of the kind of
movement that occurs in you when you are in awe, when you are
speechless, when you sense that what you are experiencing at this
moment is bigger than your life and your ability to comprehend. It
is spiritual and emotional wonder, a moment of liminality where
you are close to what you find holy. Most often those moments
occur in nature, come as a surprise, and convey a sense of God's
presence. They are truly sacred moments. Smelling God was for
me a moment of transcendence, a sacred moment that touched
every atom in my body, as I mentioned in the Introduction. I felt
strangely small and insignificant, yet totally connected to a larger
whole. I was moved.

A play-full life without being moved by transcendence is
unimaginable. Being moved by the presence of transcendence
does not always take place in nature, but it probably does include
movement. Someone's story invites you into this sacred space,
and so too does reading a book, listening to a symphony, visiting a
gallery, or entering into a historic cathedral for the first time. Transcendence finds you even as you practice transcendence. Moses
can testify to this.

He was a simple shepherd who grew up in a palace, the adopted
son of a king's daughter. What irony, a person of privilege tending
flocks. Moses is looking after his father-in-law's herd one day near
Mount Horeb, a holy mountain considered to be God's dwelling
place, when an angel appears to him. The angel does not take a
human form, but rather appears as (or in) a burning bush. Seeing
that the fire does not consume the bush, Moses moves closer. He
is curious. Moses senses that something special is happening here.
Then, in ways similar to three angelic visitors becoming one, the
angel here too becomes God. God reminds Moses that he is on
holy ground and instructs him to take off his sandals. Moses, for

the first time, meets the God of his ancestors: the "I am" who was the God of Abraham, Isaac, and Jacob. What a moment this is! In awe and fear Moses hides his face. God tells Moses about the suffering of God's people in Egypt. God was moved by tears and cries, and now instructs Moses to move too. Moses is instructed to lead God's people to a promised, spacious, and abundant land. Meeting the Transcendent, now Immanent in a burning bush, Moses goes back to Egypt to free God's people.

Awe and wonder, it seems, first bring us to a moment of immobility and insignificance before we are set in motion with renewed meaning and passion. Practicing transcendence is not as difficult as it sounds, and burning bushes are not rare bushes found only on the slopes of a holy mountain. Engage in this experiment for the next two days:

> Tomorrow, when someone asks you how you are doing, answer: "My life is really busy right now." There is a good chance that the statement accurately reflects your life at this moment, but even if not, do engage in this experiment. Answer this way every time you are asked how you are doing. You might even want to tell yourself that you are busy and have little time during the day. Just use the mantra: "I'm busy." Tomorrow evening, after a day of proclaimed busyness, touch base with yourself and take your spiritual, emotional, and relational pulse. I have done this experiment, and drawing on my experience, I imagine that your self-state will resemble the one I had: you will be cranky, short tempered, and you might feel as if you did not have enough time for your day. Your relationships could be strained. Your anger may have surprised you as you drove somewhere or as you engaged your loved ones.
>
> The following day, change your response and your self-talk to: "It's a wonderful day filled with possibility" or something similar. Repeat this to yourself a few times during the day. Tell others about your day. Again, before going to bed, take

your spiritual and emotional pulse. This time, I imagine you will be at peace with yourself. Maybe you noticed something in your immediate environment that deepened your sense of being a person intricately woven into a much larger living web. This special moment comes in the form of waking with the birds; meeting the eyes of the elderly person shuffling along the sidewalk; offering a listening ear to someone who needs it; maybe seeing the leaves of a tree catch the last rays of the day; or maybe in a message you received from God or communicated to God.

Engaging the practices of play-fullness already mentioned in this chapter prepares you to experience transcendence. In the first part of the experiment above, you were so keenly aware of the shortage of time that you denied yourself the opportunity to experience wonder and awe. Then you changed direction, making a metaphorical U-turn, and by creating space within yourself you opened yourself to experience transcendence and the Transcendent. This communication rarely comes in fantastic, out-of-this world ways such as burning bushes but through everyday occurrences, such as recognizing that the many faces you see each day remind you of the image of God alive in every person.

> How do you structure your day in such a way as to give you the best opportunity to experience transcendence?

Practicing transcendence is possible because we are spiritual beings, always. Being spiritual in our culture is often associated with engaging in magical thinking. Despite thinking of ourselves as having come of age or that we are an advanced people, magical thinking is more common than we imagine. We do not talk much about death or dying, for instance, for we are afraid that we might bring death into our reality. We say "knock on wood," believing to some extent at least that doing so wards off some form of evil, which, we firmly believe, is about to pounce on us. We think that if we bury a statue in our garden, we will sell our home faster. Or we pray to God to win the lotto or to win this soccer match or that football game.

> How do you think visiting a sacred site can enrich your life?

A play-full person prays differently, as chapter 5 argues. Magical thinking decries transcendence, for transcendence recognizes that we are part of a beautiful, sacred, yet mysterious whole that does not find us to be the center point of its reality. We cannot control or manipulate this whole by using a few words, whether the words are pious or religious or even found in Scripture. Awe and wonder does not know such manipulation. Practice transcendence by:

- Putting yourself in a position where experiencing awe, wonder, and mystery is possible

- Entering into or deepening a relationship with someone you deem Holy

- Joining a sacred community

- Seeing life as a journey

- Sitting in a thunderstorm

- Reflecting on the miracle of life

- Meditating next to a large body of water

- Spending time in a desert, a forest, or another part of nature

- Worshiping in a (Gothic) cathedral

- Participating in religious rituals

- Drawing a mandala

- Walking a pilgrimage such as Camino de Santiago de Compostela (the Way of St. James) in Spain

- Visiting ancient religious sites such as Angkor Wat in Cambodia; Egypt's pyramids; Mount Zion in Jerusalem; Machu Picchu or the Nazca lines in Peru; the National Cathedral in Washington D.C.; The Potalo Castle in Lhasa, Tibet; Stonehenge in England; and Uluru (Ayers Rock) in Australia's Northern Territory.

As a spiritual person, you are responsible for nurturing your need to experience transcendence. By practicing *realness, creativity, boundlessness, slowness,* and *hospitality,* you will notice that practicing transcendence follows as a close companion. To be moved is not only an obligation, but also a gift. Within our culture, where words are freely available and often used, experiencing moments where words are absent and ultimately unable to capture the moment takes intentionality.

In Conclusion

The fear that you may have little time to practice play-fullness is real and can paralyze you. The source of this fear, like most fears, is not necessarily external reality, but how we think about time. If you think that you do not have time to be hospitable, for example, the chances that you will become hospitable to others diminish greatly. Yet our relationship with time is deeply spiritual and emotional. As you engage some of the practices encouraged by this chapter, you may discover that practicing play-fullness is not only easier than you first imagined, but also truly life-giving.

Practicing play-fullness is always a subversive act. In the introduction we saw that to be play-full is to imaginatively and creatively engage your self, others, God, and all of reality so that peace and justice reign within you, with others, and in every conceivable situation you find yourself. This sense of peace and justice inevitably introduces you to people that most individuals and society in general avoid. Like a blind person who suddenly sees and a deaf person who suddenly hears, play-fullness leads to new discoveries about yourself, others, and a world you thought you understood. The subversive nature of play-fullness, however, does not leave oppressive structures untouched. These structures of injustice leave their mark also on us and not only on those directly influenced by powers that serve consumerism, conflict, control, and the other enemies of play-fullness. Like a child who finds joy and even empowerment in doing exactly what Mom or Dad forbid and what would likely anger them, practicing play-fullness offers us a prophetic alternative to a culture that is like a runaway train, heading faster and faster to an abyss of catastrophe leaving persons, relationships, and resources destroyed in its wake.

Within the practices of this chapter hides the promise of hope. To hope is to anticipate a reality, not present at this moment, coming toward you. It is to see with an eye that reality does not have. At the same time, you recognize that the enemies of play-fullness diminish in your life. By remaining open to the present moment and an unfolding future, you receive the gifts of promise and potential. This hopeful life is possible for you as an individual — as the next chapter argues — but also in your relationship with others and with God.

FOUR

Being Play-full When Alone

Being play-full necessitates cultivating our inner or core self in order to then be able to relate to others and be play-full with them. When we are in the process of restoring our relationship with ourselves, and are seeking a sense of meaning for our lives, a creative and imaginative life is possible. We need not arrive at some point before we can be play-full with ourselves or others. This chapter asks you to see yourself with new eyes, to empower yourself to experience freedom, and to recognize yourself as a stranger in need of hospitality. When alone, it seems, the enemies of play-fullness are especially virulent. Engaging the play-full practices discussed in the previous chapters will counter their power and presence. So in this chapter we revisit the risks of being too critical toward ourselves, too controlling, too driven in our actions of engaging in conflict and of consuming too much. But we also think of what it means to be real when alone, to be creative and boundless, to practice slowness, hospitality, and seeking transcendence. First, however, I would like to introduce you to your inner space, your inner core self.

Cultivate Your Inner Space

Christians long ago believed God had an inner space, and, since we are made in the image of God, we have one too. I appreciate how theologian Henri Nouwen writes about the space as something hidden in the center of our being, a place from which we live, where our identity is defined by God, not others. Living in the center brings us not only into the center of ourselves and the center of God, but also into the center of humanity, Nouwen states. When we live at the center, that's where we discover our neighbor, and ourselves, and where we discover that we are children of God. This knowledge, Nouwen concludes, enables God to work through us, to radiate love into the world. Our inner space is thus a spiritual, emotional, and relational place inside ourselves. The enemies of play-fullness have direct influence on the shape, size, and character of our inner spaces. Our inner space has many and diverse traits:

- It can be large or small
- It can love or it can hate
- It can feel secure or it can feel threatened
- It can experience vitality or be depressed
- It can be at peace or it can be anxious
- It can seek community or it can retreat into isolation
- It can be hospitable or hostile (angry)

Likewise, our inner spaces can be flexible, valuing, satisfied, sensual, compassionate, and enthusiastic — or not. Sometimes we love some people while hating others, splitting our inner spaces at great cost to ourselves.

What is the size and nature of your inner space?

Jesus is an example of someone who had a large inner space. Take a minute and recall some of the stories you have heard about him.... It seems as if Jesus always had room to invite another woman, child, leper, sinner, or tax collector into his life. Then he told us that we must love our enemies. He was secure in who he was, telling us that "I am...the Bread of life...the Vine...the Light for the world." There seems to be no lack of confidence in Jesus. He exuded vitality to such an extent that he attracted people to himself, especially people who struggled with illnesses or other serious concerns. When others were all riled up and about to kill him, he quietly walked through them and left town. Surrounding himself with close friends, he feasted with people so often that he was called a drunkard and a glutton. Here we also discover Jesus' hospitality, with him being a host providing food to eat and washing his guests' feet. He seemed flexible too, for he would change plans and go elsewhere if he was not wanted. When he met people, he did not judge them even when he knew about their dubious pasts. Instead he valued them as fellow sisters and brothers and invited them into a personal relationship with him.

> Name three things you can do to change your inner space to better reflect Jesus' inner space.

Yet there were some people who were not so generous in their attitudes toward him. The Pharisees tracked his every action. Their small inner spaces and their lives exhibited the opposite of what we recognize in Jesus.

> Check in with yourself often during the day to discern the size of your inner space. If it is too small to foster intimacy with others, imagine stretching your inner space. You can meditate on what a large inner space would mean for you and ask God to help you to make room for yourself or someone else.

To become play-full is to stretch our inner space to be more like that of Jesus: large, loving, secure, and vital. Yet when the enemies of play-fullness are active in our lives or when we are tired or stressed out, our inner spaces shrink and we become hostile to ourselves and to others.

Alone with the Enemies of Play-fullness

In chapter 1 we looked at six corrupted forms of play-fullness: *Criticism, control, compulsion, competition, conflict,* and *consumption.* In the discussion on criticism I mentioned that typically our biggest critic grows within us when we internalize critical and punitive authority figures, especially those from our childhoods. Remember Peter who once cultivated his father's fields and Kanisha who looks in the mirror and reminds herself that she is fat? Their inner critics were active and colored the way they experienced themselves. Having our inner critics as close companions, we are never really alone. So too, of course, we find God always being with us, God Immanuel.

> What can you do to increase your self-confidence by just 10 percent?

Being Too Self-Critical

When we are alone, *criticism* takes an overt form as it did for Kanisha or a more subtle form such as Peter's procrastination. Our inner critic can be so powerful that it becomes a filter through which we experience the entire world. Peggy is a loving mother of three active preschool boys. She dreads going grocery shopping with them for inevitably the two older boys will knock something off the shelf, open a packet of cookies, start fighting with each other, or become lost in a different aisle. Feeling that others will judge her a "bad" mother, Peggy then typically explodes at the boys.

Richard also engages the world through the lens of criticism, but for him it manifests somewhat differently. An accountant in a big law firm, his inner critic tells him constantly that he is under-valued and underappreciated. After finishing a recent project, he found himself walking past his supervisor's office many times, hoping that his supervisor would see him, call him in, and praise him for the good work he has done. It never happened, and Richard now fears that he will be laid off in the next round of company restructuring.

> When do you tend to interpret others' behavior or attitudes toward you as criticism? Engage your inner critic in dialogue before you engage the other person or persons.

When we are alone, the most common forms of criticism are:

- Experiencing guilt feelings
- Seeking perfectionism
- Procrastinating
- Emotionally becoming younger than our chronological age
- Lacking self-confidence
- Avoiding others
- Taking no risks or too many risks

When criticism is active in our inner worlds, we easily project it onto others whom we now experience as being judgmental toward us or as exposing weakness in us. First that criticism enters our language and before long we find that it is difficult to say positive things about anyone or anything. Viewing the world through a lens of criticism colors everything we do.

Control: Too Little or Too Much

In a world where most of us have very little *control* over powerful forces such as severe illness, the economy, employment possibilities, national and international security, and global warming, seeking individual control becomes an antidote to the anxiety these forces unleash in us. I'm reminded that the ancient Greeks had only one word for both poison and antidote (*pharmakos*, the root for our word *pharmacy*); one had to discern from the context whether the speaker or author was referring to poison or antidote. Seeking control in the face of powerful systemic forces poisons our souls. Remember Hailey's dad and Frank whom we met in chapter 1?

What role does control play in your life?

Linda's deep secret controls her food intake. She was five years old when she first heard her mother say with much pride: "I can still fit into the same clothes I wore when I finished high school." What began as a mother's statement of pride became a daughter's secret and burden. Images in Linda's mind of the hourglass shape of her mother kept Linda from starting a family when her friends did, opting for a career instead. But the children did come and so too did a love/hate relationship with food. Often overeating, Linda is a master at skipping meals and going on "cleansing" diets.

When you are alone, control can present itself as:

- Shaping your body in unhealthy ways
- Watching time
- Answering the phone every time it rings

- Checking your e-mail many times a day

- Changing television channels often

- Struggling with constipation

- Fighting your own thoughts

Where do you recognize yourself in this list? When control determines the way we spend our time alone, it turns everything into effort and hard labor. It also keeps our activities from being life-giving or transformative to us, because all our activities remain compliant to the control.

I Have To

Compulsion as an enemy of play-fullness shrinks your inner space while leaving you with an insatiable appetite. Looking at pornography is one activity Anton detests but cannot stop. It started a few years back during a time in which the intimacy within his marriage was not satisfactory. A friend introduced him to a "safe" porn website and soon he was a paid subscriber. With wireless Internet in his house, he placed a computer in his workshop, telling this wife he was using it to do research on home projects. At first he enjoyed the tension relief as he masturbated, but now he finds that even that activity has lost its pleasure. Despite this he returns again and again, sometimes more than once a day. Prayer has not helped him overcome his habit, but neither does the pseudo-intimacy he finds through a computer screen meet his needs for human warmth, vulnerability, and touch.

Shirley's two "I have to do it" activities seem innocent despite the isolation they bring to her life. Twice a week, Shirley gets on a free bus that takes her and many septuagenarians like her to a nearby casino. Time flies as she chases the $100,000 grand prize of the penny slot machines. Sometimes she goes over to the nickel slot machines, where the prize is $500,000, but because she uses her social security money for it, she usually feels too guilty to play anything but the penny slots. Shirley will not allow anything, including invitations from friends and even doctors' appointments, to disrupt her Tuesday and Friday casino visits. Moreover, when Shirley leaves her home, she always leaves it in chaos. She is a pack rat; stuff, mostly old and useless stuff like magazines, plastic containers, glass bottles, and expired discount coupons, are everywhere, and she has even designated some of the rooms in her house as storage rooms. Her most recent purchase from a television shopping channel was an exercise glider, but like the antelope it was named after, it moved too fast for her and she placed it in storage before she used it a second time. Cleaning — such as it is — has become easier, since most of the floor space in her home is now covered with stuff. Vacuuming is neither needed nor even possible. Because her friends avoid her home and because of her regular casino trips, Shirley knows loneliness intimately.

What harmful or hurtful behavior do you feel compelled to engage in when you are alone? What needs are met by the behavior?

Remember Corey, Dora, Yuri, Joanne, Ely, and Sandra in chapter 1 and the forms of compulsion they engaged in? Which of the following forms of overplay do you recognize in your own life?

- Engaging in ritualistic behavior
- Having repetitive thoughts or irresistible urges
- Spending too much time on social networking websites such as *Facebook, Twitter,* and *LinkedIn,* or playing endless video games
- Being consumed by a single activity or hobby
- Worrying excessively or daydreaming

- Weighing yourself every day or exercising excessively

- Dreaming sexual or voyeuristic fantasies

Compulsive behaviors greatly diminish the quality of life and relationships we have. When we are compulsive when alone, loneliness and isolation become our intimate enemies.

I'm a Winner, or a Loser

When we have to show ourselves as superior due to our *competitive* spirit, our play-full selves are undermined. *Competition* when alone often takes the form of perfectionism and the hope of false value judgments it offers. Perfectionism, however, only generates losers. Remember Ruth who continually asked her professor to allow her to rewrite her work in order to improve her grade and who measured boyfriends against potential others? Kaitlin identifies with Ruth even though they've never met.

Kaitlin is having a few girlfriends over after they have all seen their kids off to school. She decided to bake muffins using organic ingredients grown locally. Her first batch tasted great but somehow they varied in size quite a bit and she was convinced that she could not give her friends this batch to eat. Dread filled her at the thought that her next batch would turn out like the first. She walked to the cupboard and took out some store-bought biscotti just in case this batch flopped too. Then she remembered she still has to clean the mess the kids made in the living room. The dread Kaitlin is feeling is the same dread she feels when her mother visits with her. Then she cleans every corner of the house and lectures her children on being polite and obedient.

Who would you be if your perfectionism did not render you a loser?

Another destructive form of competition when alone is *envy*. Envy is also a form of unconscious conflict. More powerful than jealousy, envy goes beyond issues of sharing, ownership, or possessiveness, themes tied to being jealous. We are jealous of a friend who just got a new car while we continue to drive our clunker. Recognizing our jealousy, we joke with our friend about exchanging cars. Or we are jealous when someone else moves too close to an intimate partner and becomes a threat to our relationship. Jealousy, most often, has something specific in mind, speaks to ownership of sorts, and brings tension into our relationships.

Most of us are not aware of our envy. Envy is gratuitous aggression toward what is good because we feel that the other is withholding, or keeping himself or herself, from us. What is being withheld can be love, relationship, recognition, belonging, or a specific need. Someone is capable of meeting our need but refrains from doing so. We then tend to defend ourselves against envy by placing the person who is withholding from us in a bad light or by wishing that person ill fortune. Sometimes we idealize the person, hoping that by doing so he or she will recognize our needs. A person who is envious often becomes greedy and cannot be play-full. *A play-full life is a grateful life and envy does not know gratitude.* Rather, gratitude is the antidote to the poison of envy.

> How do you increase gratitude in your
> life to counter any envy you may have?

Tammy is one of fourteen people working together as a team in a large advertising company. Envy is affecting her relationships negatively and is consuming her life. Tammy feels she has great ideas for the team's current project, which she shared at a brainstorming session but which went unrecognized by Brenda, Tammy's project manager. This has turned Tammy into a negative person who cannot say anything positive about her supervisor, someone she'd previously called a friend. At lunches with colleagues she tries to convince them how inept Brenda is as a project manager. Not surprisingly, her colleagues now make excuses when Tammy suggests lunch. Our competitiveness is also seen in:

+ Having ambition beyond specific skills or gifts

+ Avoiding all competition or turning everyday activities into a competition

+ Finding yourself in power struggles of relationships with conflict

+ Keeping some rules while breaking others

+ Devaluing potential rivals

+ Having envy toward others

+ Being unable to collaborate or work cooperatively

I'm Hurting Myself

You already know that the enemies of play-fullness rarely remain solo. They like to team up and soon we have to face a compulsion that is also filled with *conflict*. Earlier we defined "conflict" as any behavior or action, whether verbal or nonverbal, that physically hurts others or has the potential to cause bodily, emotional, relational, or even economic harm. Remember Dad Garrett of the Travis family and his volcanic anger in chapter 1? Conflict can be a fatal attempt at intimacy as we fight against the isolation and rejection we might be experiencing. Like cowboys, we rope people in by fighting with them if we do not know any other way to establish closeness.

> What behavior do you engage in that harms your body?

Sometimes conflict joins forces with control, as is the case with Randy. Randy is an aggressive driver, though he does not like to admit it. Randy learned how to drive in Los Angeles, where, according to him, there is no choice other than being an aggressive driver. Randy now lives in Nebraska, where "home style" driving is his biggest frustration. Recently he had a major scare. When Randy cut in front of a car cruising to a red light so that he could be off first, the driver of the vehicle suddenly jumped out of his car and banged on Randy's window with a baseball bat in hand. As he spewed curses at Randy and invited him to "fight like a man," luckily for Randy the light turned green and Randy sped off, his heart pounding in his throat.

Hannah's aggression toward herself manifests itself differently. She drinks too much, combining compulsion and conflict and a number of the enemies of play-fullness in one activity. It started innocently. Her mother introduced Hannah to "G&Ts" (a gin and tonic mixed drink) while Hannah was a senior in high school. Her mom would pour her "a weak one," and while sipping they would share details of the day. It was a special time of bonding. Now in her mid-thirties, Hannah drinks mainly vodka. Though trained as a nurse, she feels the nursing field has advanced too much in recent years for her to reenter that discipline after being a stay-at-home mom. Afraid that her husband will find the empty bottles, she hides the bottles until she can discard them when nobody's around.

When you are alone, conflict might surprise you in the form of:

- Using violent language (cursing, shaming or belittling others, even some forms of satire and sarcasm)

- Breaking rules (stealing, plagiarizing, tax evasion, fraud, and more)

- Being defensive or feeling like a victim

- Refusing to engage in the process of reconciliation or forgiveness

- Using recreational or prescription drugs or other forms of self-hurt

- Attempting to commit suicide

- Being a sexual predator or putting yourself at risk in your sexual relationships

I Want More: Excessive Consumption

When we are alone, we often *consume* much, taking in excessively to address a spiritual, emotional, and relational hunger or another need. Hannah consumes too much alcohol. I sometimes eat too much as if I am also eating for tomorrow. At the local Chinese buffet restaurant, I have choices from sushi to Mongolian stir-fry to American Chinese cuisine. As is common for buffet restaurants, one can go back as many times as one wants, each time receiving a new plate, a fresh beginning. I forget often that we receive daily bread.

It was January of 1973 when I left home and "lost" my mother to go to school. It was a traumatic experience for me and soothing myself with food came naturally. Within months I went from being a skinny boy to the overweight person I am slowly growing out of as an adult.

My form of consumption causes a poor body image and has possible health risks, but other forms of consumption are equally dangerous. Aiden is a compulsive shopper. His preferred objects are designer sneakers, and he is proud to say that he owns more than 225 pairs of shoes from every major sport shoe manufacturer. Some of the shoes are now seen as collectors' items and Aiden won't wear them, for they have worth. Working part-time while finishing his undergraduate degree, he has accumulated significant credit card debt. He often feels he needs to reward himself with a new pair of shoes after he has completed some task. Aiden is concerned about his employment possibilities after hearing from friends that some employers now do background checks that include a credit history when one seeks employment.

What do you take in excessively?

When we consume too much, we become unjust. By using more resources than we need, we inevitably deprive nature or someone else of resources, for we live in a reality with limited resources. This injustice, of course, is difficult to see, since we rarely know where the raw materials we draw upon come from and what were the costs to nature and lives. We may even invent additional unjust ways to maintain our lifestyles. Play-fullness, however, seeks justice, always, and this reckons the cost of consumption. Consumption when we are alone can also be seen in:

+ Rewarding yourself often or impulse buying
+ Watching too much television or spending too much time online
+ Having many books you've never read
+ Being brand conscious
+ Engaging in any activity that "kills time" (often called a "soft addiction," such as video games)
+ Using a vehicle when walking or riding a bicycle is possible
+ Often returning goods to a store after purchasing

As you continue to grow in becoming play-full, it is important to be mindful of how powerful forces such as *criticism, control, compulsion,* and the other enemies of play-fullness inhibit your growth. *Inevitably, the presence of these enemies causes our inner spaces to shrink, sometimes to a size where we do not even have room for ourselves.* Since the enemies seem to gain strength when we are alone, the play-full practices discussed in the previous chapter are your best allies in growing toward emotional, relational, and spiritual maturity.

How would you evaluate your play-fullness when you are alone? What can you do to increase your playfulness?

Play-full Practices When Alone

The previous chapters not only describe activities that will help us grow toward play-fullness, but also provide a vision of a life that revolves around life-giving and life-affirming thoughts and actions. By practicing *realness, creativity, boundlessness, slowness, hospitality,* and *transcendence,* whether we are alone or with others, our inner spaces will grow in size, security, and love. The persons you met thus far in this chapter, folks like you, are growing away from the enemies of play-fullness. They discovered that if they can bring about healthy changes in one part of their lives, change often comes to the other parts as well. Follow the examples of the people in this chapter or find your own way to becoming more play-full when alone. A good place to begin is to ask yourself: *Am I real?*

I Am Real

Chapter 2 describes *realness* as the ability to hold paradox, resist dichotomous thinking, and view ourselves as deeply paradoxical creatures. If you embrace the fact that you have an inner space that oscillates between being large *and* being small, or that you love one moment *and* hate the next, you've already started practicing realness. When you are mindful that you can be unloving and cruel, your sharp edges, as the Skin Horse mentioned in chapter 2, become softer. Realness when you are alone has to do with mindfulness, being attentive or thoughtful, and looking into the deepest portions of your being, even those dark places you hide from everyone else.

Contemplating any of the following questions can increase your faithfulness:

+ Have I been criticizing or consuming too much?

+ When am I bored and what can I do to experience vitality?

+ What parts of me might others experience as a sharp edge?

+ How can I be vulnerable toward others?

+ Who would I be if I were more resilient than I now think?

+ In what ways am I hurting others and myself?

+ What "crazy" or disturbing thoughts do I have that I best need to contain or share only in appropriate relationships?

+ Who am I when I lose my temper or my patience?

+ How do I shape the world I live in to become a better place for tomorrow's generation?

+ In what parts of culture, including religion, do I partake?

+ How does my partner or family experience me when I retreat into isolation?

+ What would realness look like for me?

+ How do I befriend my own death?

As Peggy reflected on what it means to be real as a mom of three busy little boys, one word kept coming to her mind: *permission.* Sometimes giving herself permission to be overwhelmed by the three boys softened her critical voice, the hard edge she exposes to herself. She also recognized that the mere thought of doing grocery shopping with her boys shrinks her inner space to the size where her exploding in anger is a natural consequence. Giving herself permission to say: *I cannot do this!* went against Peggy's grain and she almost got a migraine headache. Over the years migraine headaches have been an effective way of gaining space just for herself. The men in the house know not to disturb Mom when she lies in a dark room. When her husband came home from work one evening, she told him that from now on she would not go grocery shopping with the boys and asked him to join her in coming up with a new plan.

Richard's mindfulness took him in a different direction than Peggy. He was most convicted by the question of how he is shaping the world for today's younger generation and had to admit that he is doing very little if anything to better this world. He then remembered that his company has a policy of giving time off for selected community activities, one being becoming a Big Brother. The next day he called, and soon he was meeting with Mariano, a curious but shy boy named after his mother's favorite baseball star. Mariano noticed everything about Richard, what he was wearing, whether he was a minute early or a minute late, and how many times Richard would say the word "cool." Richard's search for realness showed him that he has very few people in his inner space and the ones that reside there look like him, act like him, and have a similarly endowed bank account. As Richard befriended Mariano and became his mentor, Richard's supervisor lost prominence in Richard's life.

As you've probably noted, one play-full practice often awakens another. As Peggy and Richard deepened their sense of being real, both became creative and hospitable to themselves and to others.

How can you commit time, even just a few minutes each day, to deepening your sense of realness? What would that realness look like for you?

I'm Creative

Creativity invites you to use and nurture your imagination. It also asks of you to hold the tension your paradoxical existence brings. Finding life and meaning between the *symptoms* we bring and the *signs* reality gives us, we engage the rich world of *symbols*, where this stands for that. To be creative when we are alone thus speaks not only to activities such as painting and photography, or writing poems, journals, and playing music; it is also reflected in the mindfulness that we bring to the relationships that grow on us like moss. To be creative is impossible if we do not step into a third world that is neither purely subjective nor purely objective, but carries elements of both.

Linda wants to be more creative with her food and give up the control she feels she has to exert when it comes to her weight. In her sixties, she did not want to join a group of any kind, and fearing that she would openly blame her mother she did not feel ready to meet with a counselor, either. Linda asked herself: How can I be creative with my need for controlling my food and weight? She decided on a dual approach. First, she joined an all women's gym, where she exercises and strengthens her muscles, something she has never done before. She visits the gym four times a week before lunchtime, for she found that after working out she is not very hungry and so eats less. Also, Linda remembered a movie she saw many years ago named *Babette's Feast*. She rented it again and decided she needs to enjoy her food more, be hospitable, and learn to eat with all her senses. Since she enjoys preparing food, she committed to inviting friends for dinner. After a few weeks of visiting the gym and hosting her second dinner Linda discovered that she liked her body more and that it can do things she never thought possible. Her friends loved her food; feasting with them she discovered her attitude toward food is shifting. A side-benefit was that she was invited to dinner with her friends.

Linda found a creative way to solve her difficulty: she began exercising and cooking. In the introduction I shared that a core aspect of my play-fullness includes long-distance motorcycle travel and planning for such rides. You will have to find your own creative approach that cultivates play-fullness in you when no one is around. Experiment with the following:

- Imagine how having a larger inner space will affect your life
- Externalize your inner world, including your dream world, by journaling, painting, or writing
- Take up a new hobby or reestablish a relationship with an old one
- Seek solitude and meditate on being play-full
- Read a novel
- Talk to yourself, often, and even out loud
- Be selective as you watch television or go online

I Am Free

A play-full life is a life that knows boundlessness beyond a life of shortage or confinement. If we experience the world in terms of too little time, too little money, and too little pleasure, soon we feel imprisoned by obligation, or worse, by our own guilt feelings. Remember the boundlessness of the widow with oil and of the African violet lady? Beyond the obvious oil and flowers, both women discovered something in themselves that flowed to others: a deep sense of gratitude for a life restored and redeemed. A boundless person is one who reverberates with vitality and energy that gives life to self and others. This creative force within a play-full person makes it possible to find freedom *within* boundaries. Ironically, boundaries, especially the ones placed before us by God, do not restrict at all, but promise the very freedom for which we long.

Few things enslave as much as pornography. Anton knew this personally. Reflecting on why he goes online covertly in his shop, he thought of the mixed messages he received about sexuality growing up. He also saw a link between pornography and boredom in his life and was convinced that he has genitalized sexuality to the point where he cannot have a healthy intimate relationship with his wife. Most significantly, Anton recognized that he is limited by his inability to communicate with his wife. Frustrated by the frequency and monotonous nature of intimacy in his marriage, he escapes to pornography.

Anton went online once more, this time to seek help and accountability for his compulsion. He joined an online community that empowers people to find freedom from pornography. Following their guidelines, he did something he never thought he'd do: he removed his laptop from his workshop. That absence was difficult to sustain, but he found much encouragement in his support group. Then he covenanted to use his computer only in the presence of others, for he would never dream of going to a porn site with his wife and children around. He also downloaded software to track his Internet use and asked his best friend to be his accountability partner, giving him the password to the software package. Still unable to share his feelings and frustrations with his wife, Anton read books on how men communicate their emotions and needs. Feeling more empowered, he is wondering whether he and his wife should see a marriage counselor.

> What freedom are you looking for? What might be a solution that would take you toward that freedom?

Boundlessness, of course, speaks to how we experience space and time. Shirley recognized she was running out of space at home, and on the days she visited the casino she felt as if time was flying by. Prompted by her children, Shirley reflected on her life. She was deeply offended when she was told that her house is like the nest or midden of a pack rat. Pack rats incorporate everything and anything into their nests, including their urine. Shirley learned that middens sometimes last for thousands of years and that her children talked about razing the house after her death rather than facing its contents. The thought of the house she and her husband built nearly thirty years ago being razed was very painful for Shirley, but it forced her to admit that her house is a mess.

Shirley saw a connection between her two "loves" of gambling and storing: *anticipation*. With gambling she anticipates winning and in storing she anticipates a time of need. Identifying her struggle as one of anticipation brought less resistance to her than thinking she might be addicted to gambling or that she is a pack rat. She wondered whether she could nurture her need for anticipation in a more life-giving way. Three thoughts came to her: First, she needs to anticipate possibly moving into a retirement community and made an appointment with a financial planner. Second, if she wants to move, she has to get the house ready for prospective buyers. That means getting new paint on the walls and replacing the carpet. Of course, her stuff will have to go, maybe into a storage unit, to charity, or into a dumpster. Third, there is a local church that has a Wednesday night dinner followed by bingo. Since some of her friends already attend these evenings, she will use that to address her need for anticipation too.

As you seek play-fullness, grant yourself the freedom to accept that for the majority of life's difficulties, simple solutions are possible. Play-fullness, however, is not primarily concerned with labels or even diagnoses, but rather seeks a quality of life that permeates all our relationships.

I Slowed Down

In the classic tale, the tortoise won the race against the hare not by racing, but by being slow and deliberate. One can imagine that the hare was in a frenzy seeing the tortoise crossing the winning line first.... *Slowness* encourages you to do things at the right speed, to savor the tastes, smells, sights, and sounds of life, to touch life gently and not to rush through time and space. It resists the Fast Life, where everything is readily accessible like in a drive through.

What do you learn from the tortoise about winning the race of life?

As Kaitlin was unpacking the store-bought biscotti, she was struck by the fact that she does not even know where the biscotti was made. The label merely stated: A product of Italy. As she was mixing her second batch of batter, Kaitlin's sense of dread returned as she recognized that she would not be ready when her friends arrive. Her vision of having the smell of fresh muffins filling the house when her friends enter will not materialize. She poured herself a cup of herbal tea and worked on the new batter. She also talked to herself, telling herself that her fears do not honor the friendship and trust she has in her relationship with her girlfriends. She also had to talk back to her inner critic who was becoming louder by the minute. Putting the biscotti aside, she walked to the living room and brought her tea set back into the kitchen, reflecting on how foolish it was of her to have all these irrational fears. Suddenly the doorbell rang and her friends entered. Kaitlin beckoned them into the kitchen just as she was putting the muffin pan into the oven. As the fresh smell of baking muffins filled the air, her friends commented on how "homey" the moment was.

When alone, what would slowing down look like for you?

The fruit of play-fullness includes a sense of peace and justice toward others: the experience of restored relationships and granting others the fullness God offers them. Envy, in turn, breeds hostility. Tammy became more mindful of replacing her criticism of others with affirmations, recognizing the unique contributions every person on her team brings. What she found worked best for her, however, was to meditate daily on what a life of gratitude means for her. At first she found the reflection difficult, for she saw much of her life in terms of her "rights" or of "how things should be." As she identified numerous things she has taken for granted in her life, Tammy's strong sense of entitlement fueled by an even deeper sense of insecurity became clear to her. This insecurity has caused her to charge up the corporate ladder, believing that she will feel secure if she receives a title. With a sense of relief Tammy decided she was tired of the race.

How can you embody gratitude when you are alone? Notice how your envy diminishes as you express gratitude.

First, she reduced the amount of work she did at home, which inevitably meant putting her laptop away in the evening. Then, instead of driving her car to work and getting frustrated in rush hour traffic, she used public transportation and listened to an audio book. She decided to take a long walk every other day and eat a brown bag sandwich at her desk when she returns. On those walks she was struck by how many people were homeless and how many had focused and stern faces as they rushed past her, not even noticing her. She identified things she's grateful for, such as financial security, an education, and health, but also relationships and friendships. She sought ways to express her gratitude, thanking God and inviting some friends for dinner. Team meetings of course continued to take place, but now rather than simply offering her own ideas she adds to comments already made, improving the concepts and ideas of others. The feeling that Brenda, her supervisor, was withholding something from her, a previous itch under her skin in constant need to be scratched lessened greatly.

To live into play-fullness, we need to find ways to slow down and minimize forces such as perfectionism and envy in our lives. Increase your chances of living at the right pace by:

- Visiting the library two hours a week just to read

- Talking with God more often, including praying regularly

- Meditating on the meaning of gratitude

- Increasing your tolerance for dirt and chaos

- Teaching a family dog new tricks

- Folding origami figures

- Researching and cooking one "exotic" meal each week

- Granting yourself a visit to a massage therapist once a month

I Am Making Room for Myself

We noted earlier that Jesus was hospitable. *Hospitality* calls on you to create space for yourself and others where they and you can grow. This space is filled with potential. Remember the biblical story of three visitors who became One? Of course, when we think of hospitality, we often think of opening our home to friends or maybe strangers. To love yourself, however, to live into the moral and ethical mandate Jesus gave you, is also a form of hospitality.

With vivid images in his head of what the guy with the base-ball bat could have done to his car or, worse, his head, Randy thought about his tendency to cut in front of other drivers when he approaches a red light. He was not even five yet when he discovered that to be first is very important. He started playing tennis at that time, showed some potential, and his parents and Coach Lessing all said they expected great things from him. Dad's reminding him of the expense of his tennis lessons did not help. What Randy took away from all those years of coaching was: Be a winner! However, he was not that good and lacked a winning instinct. "Winning" when behind the wheel came easier than winning a tennis match, and thus he has always been a very aggressive driver. As Randy pondered disappointing his coach and parents in not becoming a winner, deep emotion overcame him. First he felt shame that he had never produced what others thought he could. Then he felt helplessness set in, followed by rage — that generalized emotion deeper than anger with no specific object in mind. It is rage that comes to him when driving and rage he recognized in the eyes of the guy with the baseball bat. Randy at last understood that he has to be hospitable to that part of him he'd rather forget: being a child or teenager who feels he disappointed Mom, Dad, and Coach Lessing.

How do you become hospitable to that part within yourself that can be emotionally younger than your chronological age?

Hannah, after receiving a driving while intoxicated citation, recognized she needed help. She never thought of her decision to enter an addictions unit as a way of being hospitable to herself, but she knew that she could not get out of Dr. Vodka's grip alone. She tried many times and each time she failed, burdened by even more guilt feelings for living a life of deception. Her citation became a sign of hope since it exposed her dark secret and forced her to seek help. As Hannah reached out for help, she became hospitable toward her humiliation, shame, and regret, since all her family and friends — people she hurt deeply — now know her deep secret. Being hospitable to her emotional and relational world opened Hannah to receive care and support from others, something she needs as she wrestles with the question of whether she can trust and love herself again.

Making room for yourself is a spiritual mandate. It is also a gift you give yourself. Having read thus far into the book, you have discovered many practices, most of which will increase hospitality toward yourself.

I Experience Wonder

Transcendence is the practice of play-fullness that summons you to experience wonder and awe. *Awe is that deep awareness that one is small and insignificant or that one is experiencing something truly special or amazing.* It awakens within us a deep sense of respect, admiration, and gratitude. Wonder is different from awe. *Wonder is that feeling of surprise and admiration after experiencing beauty, the unexpected, or the inexplicable.* In wonder we can even be bewildered or we become curious. Curiosity leads us toward a need to understand and causes us to analyze the parts that make a whole. Wonder, however, is more passive as we recognize the experience is beyond comprehension and we are rendered speechless by the sense that the whole is bigger than the parts. To experience wonder reminds us that we are spiritual beings, longing to be reunited with our Creator. *One can argue that wonder is an act of seeing the Divine, which causes us to see the world with new eyes.* By engaging in play-fullness, we put ourself in a position where we experience transcendence, awe, and wonder.

Recall, in as much detail as possible, the last time you experienced a sense of wonder.

The practice of transcendence functions as a catalyst for growth and change. The experience I shared with you in the opening pages of this book, where I described smelling God, was a profound experience of wonder, an experience in which I became an insignificant part of a much larger whole. *How can I allow the transformative experience of wonder to help me to eat less?*

Portions of this book were written in my favorite Chinese restaurant, where a cornucopia of smells fill my awareness. A person might argue that someone who tends to eat too much should not spend time in buffet restaurants. That person would have a valid point. The restaurant, however, is a hospitable place, allowing me to stay for as long as I need to and never rushing me out the door. Typing away on my laptop, I would play with the thought that since God is found in the smell of a freshly washed pine forest, God surely must be somewhere between the smell of General Tso's chicken, chicken with cashews and vegetables, and freshly cut watermelon. As my nose searches for God, I'm struck by how little I know of the people preparing my meal. Chefs, their faces red from their stoves, bring in food to feast on. We never communicate with each other. I want that to change. As I search the air, wondering if God is in a smell, I discover the face of God in the many patrons who also enjoy the feast prepared for them. In this restaurant, the face of God is African American, Caucasian, Asian, Hispanic, able-bodied and disabled, trim and fat, large and small. And I am part of that face. As wonderment sets in, I eat with all my senses and discover one plate of food is enough. No need for seconds today. The hospitality I received invited me to see the face of God.

In all the faces you see today, discover the face of God.

Aiden recognized that spending more money on shoes is irresponsible. Urged on by friends, he went to the college counseling office wondering whether he is addicted or something. His fears were relieved and the counselor suggested that Aiden, with her help and support, find healthy ways to manage his anxiety and his finances. Later, a friend asked Aiden where God was in his experience. He was stunned by her question for he never thought about God. Unable to find an answer to her question that did not feel defensive, he made an appointment with a family friend who is a pastor. Aiden was somewhat disappointed when the pastor did not even attempt to answer his question of what God would want Aiden to do with the shoes he bought. Rather, Aiden was asked to engage in "an experiment." The pastor invited Aiden to wear a different pair of sneakers each day, including the ones he had never worn before, and to use his lunch hour to walk to the various churches around town, enter, and spend fifteen minutes reflecting on his question.

Not wanting to disappoint someone he looked up to, Aiden went off to the first church. It was the college chapel, a large Gothic building. On this first day of the experiment, he wore the latest pair of shoes he had bought. Aiden was surprised how big the chapel was with no one there to worship. Despite his sneakers his footsteps were loud, and he was conscious of the noise he was making. Aiden chose a pew near the front and sat down. Two things surprised him: first, the fifteen minutes felt awfully long; and second, he received no message or anything from God. Leaving disappointed, he returned the next day wearing a different pair of sneakers. He chose the same pew as the day before and surveyed the intricate detail of the building. He noticed a swallow's nest close to the roof in one corner and wondered when the bird had built the nest. Time passed faster than the day before, yet no answer to his questions came. Believing that the chapel must be able to offer him some wisdom, Aiden returned to the chapel day after day, empowering himself to change the experiment slightly.

Wearing his seventh pair of shoes and by now knowing the inside of the chapel in detail, Aiden felt it. Suddenly it dawned upon him that his life is as empty as the chapel he has frequented. Sneakers cannot fill the void he feels, and he has neglected his financial stability, his relationships with friends, and definitely his relationship with God. Feeling small and insignificant, he grasped that there is more to his life than he is currently experiencing. Powerful emotions flooded him. At the same time he felt utterly alone, yet strangely connected to God, even to the swallow that never came. He felt guilty, but also a sense of forgiveness; he felt bound but also free; helpless but also empowered; weak but also strong; fear but also peace. He began to sob, not knowing the reasons why, yet he was strangely comfortable with it. Leaving the chapel, he called the pastor stating: "I know what to do." Aiden felt no need to elaborate and the pastor did not ask for clarification. In his daily journal he wrote:

> I've been going to the chapel seven days in a row. At first I was confused about what the experiment was all about. And then to wear a different pair of sneakers every time I do so, was it a weird kind of punishment? I knew the experiment was not about the chapel, but about a possible relationship between God and my sneakers. At first I thought: God does not want me to have sneakers. Then I thought: I need to give my sneakers away. Then: I cannot be a good person and have all these sneakers. Then I went to: What sneaker would Jesus wear? And why did Moses take off his shoes when he met God at the burning bush? Then: Who made the sneakers I am wearing today? Then I thought: Maybe I can sell the sneakers and give the money to charity or give them away as birthday gifts. These thoughts were interesting, but not compelling. My final thought was: My life is as empty as the chapel and God and relationships can fill the void. I think I am going to sleep well tonight. Like Moses who took off his shoes at the burning bush, I can take off my sneakers, for I have discovered I am on holy ground.

Place yourself in a position to experience wonder:

- Experience silence for ten to twenty minutes or more each day
- Listen to sacred music

- Allow your eyes to rest on something larger than yourself, such as the night sky or a mountain vista, or possibly something much smaller than you, such as the intricacies of a spider's web
- Venture safely outside in a storm
- Take a photograph of the same object every day
- Watch waves roll in only to crawl back into themselves
- Meditate on wonder or awe or spend time in prayer

In Conclusion

I imagine that you have recognized yourself in the people you met in this chapter. *We all host the enemies of play even as we long for a play-full life.* And then we question whether we have enough time to practice play-fullness. The practices of play-fullness do not necessarily require time. They require commitment. Switching off the radio or mp3 player when you drive or walk somewhere can make room for you to discern your inner space and play-fullness. You may find that even a few minutes of meditation take you to a space powerful enough to inform the rest of your day. When you commit to nurturing play-fullness within you, you will find surprising results, one of which is the release of creative, vital energy within you. You will also discover that the energy is intimately tied to some of the deepest wounds you've received and the enemies of play-fullness you harbor.

When we experience emotional, relational, or even spiritual hurt and alienation, we place those moments in a metaphorical deep freeze where they become frozen moments. As long as we expend much energy, the hurt, now frozen solid, is bearable and hidden. However, we expend so much of our energy keeping it frozen that we have no vitality; we have no emotional, relational, or even spiritual energy left to love our neighbors as we love ourselves. Practicing play-fullness inevitably thaws these frozen moments. This thawing is not without initial discomfort, but as it happens, creative and vital energy is released. Imagine the energy that went into a symptom now stretching your inner space to be more hospitable or enriching your relationships. This thawing process has started within you as you meditated on smelling God, slowing down, and seeking peace.

To be play-full when alone is an important aspect of wholistic maturity. It is thus worth cultivating. The scholar and mystic Meister Eckhart said nearly eight hundred years ago that if we tend to the birth within us — that is, when we cultivate our inner spaces — goodness, delight, being, and truth will come to us. If we seek that cultivation and growth from without, he continued, it will come to nothing, despite our efforts. Now that we are committed to being playful when alone, being play-full with others follows naturally.

FIVE

Being Play-full with Others

Often, being play-full with others is more pleasurable, gratifying, and rewarding than being play-full when alone. Furthermore, being play-full with others promotes, sustains, and deepens loving and intimate relationships. And sometimes play-fullness can even get us unstuck and save the day. For years my wife dreamed of traveling to Paris, and as a couple we have had a few failed attempts of doing so. Likewise, I anticipated for a number of years a motorcycle trip to Alaska's North Slope as I continue my dream toward circumnavigating the globe on a motorcycle. For some reason, or possibly because of these divergent dreams, both became reality the same summer. It was decided that my wife's trip would be first.

Families, generally, do not do entrances and exits well. Whether it is waking up or falling asleep, returning from or leaving for work, school or vacations, or births and deaths, transitions heighten our anxiety. Feeling the tension, the enemies of play-fullness show themselves. Every parent knows the frustration of needing to get the children off to school and one refusing to cooperate. Especially in such times being play-full is a gift. As our two daughters — aged five and three at the time — sensed that departures were imminent, and as my wife and I were aware that we would not be able to rely on each other for parenting, loving, and more, the tension in our household increased exponentially. That my trip had an element of danger added to the stress. Our daughters became "stubborn" and generally "uncooperative," and my wife and I became more irritable and impatient, even with each other. The potential for disastrous goodbyes stared us in the face.

It was at this point that we decided to add another language to our household: "*French!*" The fact that none of us could speak French was no deterrent even if it was slightly confusing. I invited our daughters to speak "French" by making verbal intonations and sounds mimicking the way I've heard French being spoken in movies and during previous travels. For a brief minute puzzlement reigned when I asked our daughters: *Parlez-vous? Mamma adieu Paris! Mula joie de vivre Papa?* I continued with another nonsense sentence or two inviting a reply from our daughters. That I randomly used words and phrases, most not even French and others totally out of context, was of little concern.

It was our oldest daughter who first responded in "French" and soon all four of us conversed in our new language around the kitchen table. As we played with sounds, we discovered that we could communicate much without knowing a language. We laughed and the tensions between us greatly diminished. Later that week, when my wife joined her friend in Paris, my daughters and I spoke "French" often.

Being play-full with language brought laughter and release, even a sense that everything would be okay. It restored a much-needed balance. Although our daughters obviously missed their mom, and I likewise my intimate partner, the days passed faster than we imagined with no changes in our daughters' eating or sleeping patterns or in their behavior, and with me being more patient and present to our daughters than anticipated. Single parenting, especially, but all parenting is unimaginable without play-fullness! You rarely have to become angry or frustrated with a child or someone else if you invite the child or person into your inner space and engage in play-full experiences.

I assume that having come this far in the book you have a good sense of how the enemies of play-fullness function in your own life and how they diminish your life and relationships. This chapter addresses how practicing *realness, creativity, boundlessness, slowness, hospitality,* and *transcendence* with others can inform your life. Again you will discover how others have been play-full. Let their creativity and sense of adventure enrich your life.

Practicing Realness with Others

Realness, you recall, challenges you to hold paradox, resist black and white thinking, and to view yourself as a deeply paradoxical being. The Velveteen Rabbit (see chapter 2) discovered that realness happens in relationship with others. It occurs naturally when you allow others to love you. Every person carries the seeds of realness, for without love, a helpless baby does not survive. A friend and professional musician, Michael, is play-full and real. He holds the paradoxes of life whether he sings about a boy born with Down syndrome, a teenager disabled in a car wreck, a friend dying of HIV/AIDS, or his driving his dying Dad to a physician. One time, he told me, he was performing in New Orleans when an aged black man listening to him approached him and said: "Man, you are watered." Not having had a drink but being Irish, Michael thought the man meant he was inebriated, until he was told the expression meant it was obvious that someone loved him deeply. The man recognized the nature of Michael's inner space.

> Who has watered you? Who is watering you at this moment? Whom are you watering?

To allow others to love you is a risk some people cannot take, especially if others touched their lives violently and restoration and healing never came. For people who are lonely, being loved by a dog or a cat, or knowing that God loves them can be the reclamation of a love they once knew. When others love us, we are pulled into the community that is shaped around us. This sense of community, too, fosters realness in us, since by its very nature community is paradoxical. We discover this in Scripture when Jesus describes the church as a bride preparing herself for her Bridegroom, who is Christ. But this bride is not always the bride set apart, patiently waiting. No, there are many images from Scripture to suggest that this bride chases other idols. Also, this is a bride who also bites and devours, as Paul warns the church in Galatia. Thus, as others love us, we hold the tension that no love is perfect. We experience joy and warmth, but also the pain of betrayal and disappointment. When the paradox of community cannot be held, community breaks down as we retreat to isolation and alienation. We just have to notice our society's high divorce rate to know that this is happening often. Being real means we commit to community and communion even though we know that we will experience disappointments, rejections, and even betrayals.

Even as love and community foster realness, no realness exists without discovering that the flesh-and-blood person we love or have just met is not the same person who we think the person is. Since we internalize relationships, we invite the persons we love and hate into our inner spaces, where they become mental images or representations. Realness thus embraces the fact that the person you married or with whom you are in an intimate relationship is not an internalized representation, a preconceived notion, or an image or vision for which you long. The recognition that an image is never a person is challenging, for that means your intimate partner, your parents, your family, your friends and acquaintances, and even strangers or your enemies are not the persons you think they are. A play-full self is never satisfied with mental images but seeks deepening relationships with persons who likewise can grow in realness.

After four years of marriage, Phil is restless and is distancing himself from his wife. Approaching thirty, he thought that he'd be settled in his career and that he and his wife would have a passionate intimate relationship. That was his dream. The reality, however, is that he is earning much less than he thinks he is worth, and he feels sexually starved. None of his fantasies of his being ravaged by his wife have come true. After speaking with his friends at the racquetball club, he wonders whether divorcing before they have children would be the prudent thing to do. Phil is unable to tell his wife of his frustrations. It is as if nothing in life prepared him to share his deepest longings with his wife. Small surprise that there is little if any play-fullness in his life or marriage. Deciding not to follow his friends' recommendation to seek another partner, Phil asked himself: If my wife is not the seductive woman who resides in my head, then who is she? Reversing the question, he mustered the courage one evening to ask her: "Did I turn out to be the husband you thought I'd be?" To his shock he heard: "Not really ... I thought you'd share your inner world with me. I never know what you think. Also, I do not really know your passions and dreams at this moment and may not have a good idea about your frustrations." Play-fullness in intimate relationships and the realness it requires ask us to relate to our partners as persons and not as internalized images. Inevitably we need to have significant conversations with our partners or ask someone else, such as a counselor, to lend us the courage to converse beyond fantasies of short-lived pleasure or experiences of long-term disappointment.

> How have you discovered your intimate
> partner to be different from the person
> residing in your head?

Realness in family relationships is often difficult to find. Phyllis thought she was a loving and supportive mother but was shocked when her daughter informed her that she is lesbian and has entered into an intimate relationship with another woman. The daughter Phyllis wanted and internalized was heterosexual and would give her a son-in-law and many grandchildren. Phyllis soon recognized that unless she discovers her daughter anew, she is not going to have any relationship of significance with her. Also, she had no idea how to tell her friends, for their daughters had seemingly great marriages and growing families. She even wondered whether she had done something wrong in raising her daughter that could have caused the lesbianism. The result was that Phyllis distanced herself from her daughter, rarely speaking with her. She did not know anything about her daughter's passions and dreams, her disappointments and hurts. Sundays were especially difficult, for Phyllis often invited her children and grandchildren for lunch, but she could not get herself to invite her daughter with her new partner. Feeling uninvited, Phyllis's daughter had one excuse after another not to attend the family meal. Phyllis discovered that our internal images of persons could prevent play-fullness with others. Living according to internal representations rarely leads to authentic selves and authentic community.

Question your internalized images and practice realness with others by:

♦ Being resilient and vulnerable in intimate relationships

♦ Finding ways to be play-full and overcome criticism

♦ Recognizing conflict and distance in relationships and seeking forgiveness and reconciliation

♦ Deepening intimacy while growing beyond two-dimensional relationships (as can be found in pornography or some forms of social networking and online relationships)

♦ Being responsive to the needs of others and containing your reactivity to "spill over" (see chapter 2)

♦ Singing in a choir, acting, dancing with others, or participating in culture

♦ Entering into and building relationships, including with persons who do not look like you, think like you, or act like you

The ultimate challenge of realness with others, however, is not necessarily intimate relationships, but dying well. Death may just be the ultimate *other,* someone or something we see as either an enemy or a friend. Befriending our own deaths speaks to a special kind of relationship. It is thus no surprise that play-full persons die differently compared to persons who lack play-fullness. Most of us will die not according to our belief system as we might think, but according to the nature of our inner spaces.

If our inner spaces are small and feel insecure, we will spend thousands of dollars to extend our lives by a few weeks or months. We will be unable to speak with our family and loved ones about our fears, unable to ask them to come around us like moss, protecting us, comforting us, even lending us some of their inner strength. Friends carry us when we lack the strength to do so. Sometimes I wonder what would happen if the dollars spent in the last month of one's life could be used to fund a school in a developing country, for example. Or if the money were to be spent rebuilding homes and lives after a devastating natural disaster or replenishing trees cut down in some remote rain forest to feed our need for exotic hardwoods. Befriending one's own death is difficult if one's faith system sees death as the enemy, something to be conquered. The empty tomb of Christ may have symbolic meaning richer than merely overcoming death. It may be an invitation into a new life, perhaps even a life that befriends death, a life that loves an enemy, even if that enemy is death.

How do others recognize in you that you will die well?

Realness with others, an integral part of becoming play-full, is an invitation to a journey of discovery and uncovering, of newness and of letting go of internal images burdening and bringing distance to your relationships. Realness requires a sense of trust, courage, and a growing inner space, but promises a deepening of our relationship with others and ourselves. Realness with others gifts us with play-fullness. We receive a similar gift if we practice creativity with others.

Practicing Creativity with Others

We practice creativity when we hold the paradoxes of being real. We also do so when we enter into that space filled with potential between our own inner worlds and perceived objectivity. Speaking "French" when nobody knows the language is being creative with others. So too is inviting persons into a "third world" not determined by economic development or politics, but inspired by the presence of imagination (see chapter 2). Play-full persons not only seek ways to practice creativity with others; they also awaken the imagination and creativity in others. Two forms of creative play-fullness might be more important than many others. Since Jesus reached out to children, we too need to be concerned about children. They are not the next generation, but the *current* one! Play-full parenting or mentoring is thus essential to a play-full life. Second, creative play-fullness with others awakens hope in people who know despair, dejection, and disappointment intimately. How can we have life to the fullest if apathy and shame, those close allies of despair and hopelessness, are present in our lives?

One certain place where creativity with others is needed is play-full parenting. When we as parents resort to "power over" our children or loved ones, we often find ourselves in a stalemate position that fosters frustration, anger, and resentment, not only in us, but also in our children. Imagine: A five-year-old screams at her mother: "I hate you, and you do not love me!" One mother, her inner space feeling small and insecure, responds:

Don't you dare use that language with me! You know that what you say is not true! If I hear you say those words again ... When your dad comes home, I'll tell him what you said. He'll give you a good spanking. . . . "

The child, probably feeling like a snail at this moment, pulls back deep into her shell or becomes prickly and defiant in order to defend herself. Another mother, her inner space large and secure, responds:

> Honey, you must be very mad or frustrated or disappointed or annoyed at me for you to say that you hate me and that I do not love you. I do not understand what you feel. But I am grateful that you tell me you hate me and that you feel I do not love you. Would you help me do something special?

Whereas the first scenario has the certainty to repeat itself often, the second carries the potential for deepening relationships and a mother creating space for her daughter to grow. Here, play-fullness allowed the mother to respond (and not react) in a way her daughter did not expect. She empowered her daughter to be confident and authentic in her relationships, even if she still lacks the ability to express herself in ways that can deepen her intimacy with others.

The path of conflict, always, is well trodden, and we can expect that the "power over" approach will foster resistance, also a form of power. One small, insecure inner space produces another. But in the same way, a secure, loving inner space births security and confidence in others. For many of us who grew up with various versions of "spare the rod and spoil the child" or "children should be seen and not heard," power over children and showing children the mistakes they make come easy. For us, play-full parenting will require much intentionality, for resorting to physical punishment or claiming power over requires no creativity, but is natural to our reactivity. Play-full parents help prevent moments that can escalate to conflict and violence. If we practice creativity with others, conflict is difficult to imagine, and the tensions we will feel will not be the tension of hostility and distancing, but the tension of connection, anticipation, and wonder. Play-full parenting assures the emotional and relational well-being of our children and fosters deep connections. It asks of us to plan less for our children, to clear their schedules so that they engage in spontaneous play and spend time to explore the world in which they live.

Psychologist Lawrence Cohen urges those who desire *playful parenting* to seek closeness with children and teenagers instead of isolation, to empower confidence instead of powerlessness, and to foster emotional recovery for a child or teenager when emotional distress remains. To do this, you need to accept and contain strong feelings in you and the child or teenager. Empower girls and connect with boys, Cohen recommends. He says one tantrum preventer he uses is having a "giggle-fest." He invites everyone to pretend laugh until all are really laughing. Doing something different almost always works. Instead of a "time-out," Cohen recommends "meeting on the couch" and other acts of connection. He writes of a mother who decided not to talk for three days after the death of a friend and found her teenage son more talkative than ever. Her silence created a space for her and her son to connect. How can you increase your connection with your children or another child? How can you empower and become the recipient of powerful emotions?

Who would you be if play-full parenting, mentoring, or even play-full intimacy were to determine your intimate relationships?

Grow in being a play-full parent:

+ Spend more time at eye-level with children, so get down on your knees or sit down on the floor and refrain from looking down upon persons smaller than you.

+ Do anything different when you feel stuck: Sing your communication; tell your child you need to walk three times around the house first or that what you need to say is so important you need to say it under the dining room table. Say: "Thank you for sharing all that your brother did to you. He obviously hurt you and I see you are very upset. But I do not want to know what your brother did...."

- Play catch, board games, video games, or draw together. Go camping or sledding or go to the pool.

- Find every opportunity to foster *connection:* Redirect words that harm and undesirable actions: "Ah, I'm an idiot! Well, you know what that means! I need to give you a hug and a kiss!" Chase after your child without catching him or her; "So, you hate me.... Now I'll have to tell you your birth story again, for the day you were born was a special day"; Feeling so angry that you may physically lash out at your child, try this: "I feel like spanking you, but before I can do that I need to catch you and tickle you until both of us have tears in our eyes, then we need to walk backward from my bedroom to yours; then we have to jump five times on your bed; then we need to exit your bedroom with me blindfolded and you leading me back to the kitchen. Only then, if I still feel like it, will I spank you. So first I need to catch you and tickle you until both of us have tears in our eyes...." When the laughter stops and the relationship has deepened, set down appropriate boundaries or consequences for your child.

- Get into a pillow fight or wrestling match with your teenager (provide just enough resistance, usually let the child win, and do not tickle the child against their will); leave small notes communicating a sense of empowerment ("You are so courageous, I know you can do it!"), care ("Remember to take a few deep breaths before the race begins. Spot me in the crowd as the proudest parent!"), and love ("I love you!"). Use *Twitter* or *Facebook* to connect with your teen and invite him or her for breakfast; laugh together.

- Notice and be attentive to your child's life: accomplishments, friends, etc. Since "good" attention wards off a child's seeking "bad" attention, say things like: "Now how did you manage to get all dressed by yourself this morning? And your hair! B-E-A-U-T-I-F-U-L!!" Or to your teenager: "Honey, you made me so proud when I saw your school report. To think you are that clever despite having tons of my genes...."

* Reverse the family roles: Children become the adults and Mom or Dad or both become the child or teenager or family pet. Keep safety in mind.

Awakening *hope* in others is a proven way to practice creativity with others and to bring a sense of peace into someone's life. Hoping, you may remember, is anticipating a reality not present at this moment, coming toward you. Hope always invites us into the space between the already and the not yet. When the enemies of play-fullness are present, whether as *criticism, control, compulsion, competition, conflict,* or *consumption,* hope diminishes greatly or is even absent. When we awaken hope in others, we change the way we talk with them. Rather than spending all our time exploring the history of a problem, or asking the person how they understand their problem, or talking about facts or medical information, diagnoses and prognoses, or even asking, "How do you feel?" ask:

* I'm curious: when or where is your [problem / name the concern] not a problem?

* Where does your [problem] bother you the least?

* If your [problem] were not present, what would a new vision for your life look like?

* How have you managed all these months with your [problem] without totally unraveling?

* What can you do to improve your life just a bit?

* How will others notice your progress or that you have gained hope?

* How will you pray (or experience God or read Scripture) differently if your [problem] no longer defines you?

Giving someone hope may not be possible, but we certainly can *awaken* hope in others. By asking persons questions such as the ones above, we invite them to open themselves to a changed reality. Persons can answer the questions only by naming strengths and positive scenarios. Naming strengths you possess but did not acknowledge and imagining a transformed life automatically awakens transforming hope in you.

Hoping, of course, is not the same as wishing. Wishing is an activity that does not require much creativity and one in which we often engage. The big difference between hoping and wishing is that, whereas hoping leaves some ambiguity and uncertainty and even openness to an alternative vision, *wishing knows exactly what it wants*. If we say: "I hope to get a new car soon," or, "I hope the weather will be fine tomorrow," we are actually wishing. Rather, say: "Whether the sun shines or it rains tomorrow, let's make it a fun-filled day. What would you like to do?" Hope carries some uncertainty for we do not exactly know how God is going to enter into our reality. A play-full person recognizes the defensive grandiosity that demands an outcome, as if persons and nature and God can be manipulated to grant our wishes. Wishing turns God into an idol. Hoping recognizes that God is always with us, in good times and in times that ask for hope to be awakened in us.

Awaken hope in another person by asking something different, such as: *If wishing knows exactly what it wants and hoping anticipates a changed future, what are you hoping for?* Or, *What keeps you from falling into the depths of despair?*

Practicing play-full creativity with others, as was evident in describing play-full parenting and awakening hope in others, requires *responsiveness* in our relationships. Due to the way our brains function, however, we most often become reactive, especially when we are anxious or when our minds interpret a situation as dangerous. Since reactivity is natural for us, responsiveness is a commitment we make to the mindfulness inherent to play-full living.

Practice creativity with others by:

* Engaging in play-full parenting

* Sharing your emotional, spiritual, and relational self with others

* Expressing compassion, the ability to "feel with" someone else, or empathy, the ability to imagine yourself in someone else's shoes

* Allowing the creativity of others to shape and transform your creativity

* Having a music evening where you play a few of your favorite songs and tell your friends why you like the songs. Invite them to share how they heard the music

* Playing board games and card games with family and friends

* Participating in building a Habitat for Humanity house or other volunteer community projects

Most practices of creativity with others will give us a sense of boundlessness, for as we spend time with friends and family, time itself will be suspended and an evening together feels like an hour.

Practicing Boundlessness with Others

I said that the desire for boundlessness that we embody comes directly from God in whose image we're made. The boundlessness is part of our play-fullness and always flows toward others, just as the African violet queen's flowers adorned many people's homes. Since vitality and energy are inherent to feeling bound-less, when those dynamic forces in our lives touch others' lives, play-fullness abounds. In chapter 2 I wrote that experiencing life as flowing, abundant, and unfailing despite the inevitable limits of an embodied existence is possible. Few experiences describe this boundlessness of being with others in as peaceful and just a way as extending or receiving forgiveness.

Forgiveness contemplates the hurt one received from someone else or from a group and remembering it differently, for erasing it from your memory is not possible. It is having a willed change of heart that overcomes hurt, anger, hatred, and resentment. You let go of the desire for retaliation and revenge. Forgiveness is a *process* of mutual encounter, self-discovery, and the reintegration of your self around new values and practices even as it is *an act*, some-thing you do. Also, it is a process *within* you and *between* you and others as a product of emotional, spiritual, and relational work. The boundlessness of forgiveness promises new meaning for your-self and for others since it redeems, reconciles, transforms, and instills hope. Despite the hard work it takes to forgive someone else, forgiveness is ultimately a gift of grace from God, touching all lives involved.

Forgiveness has many faces. The Truth and Reconciliation Commission and the peoples of South Africa amaze us as forgive-ness is extended to perpetrators of unmentionable violence. We look up to the Amish of Nickel Mines, Pennsylvania, who forgave the man who killed five of their daughters before he committed suicide. As the grieving parents and community reached out to the family of the murderer, the world watched in awe. But not all acts of forgiveness catch the world's attention:

+ A three-year-old looks his parents in the eye and then continues drawing on the wall. His parents remove him from the room and give him a time-out. They show him the newsprint he can use and ask him whether he would like to send his grandparents a piece of art. He is excited about this possibility and later he remains close to his parents, hugging both Mom and Dad in an act of reparation.

- An eight-year-old comes home with a new pen. Confronted by her parents, she says she picked it up at school. Her parents wonder aloud whether someone is missing a pen. She returns to school and hands in the pen at the Lost and Found.

- A teenager yells at his younger sister and calls her a "muffin top" (someone whose flab spills over his or her waistband). She retreats to her room in tears. Later he says: "I'm sorry I made you cry. I was mean. I'm sorry. . . . Please forgive me."

- In an act of rage, a husband cursed and lifted his hand against his wife. Other times he was a perpetrator of marital rape. Together they talked with a counselor about shame as well as power and control in their marriage. He joined a group where men are holding him accountable for this thoughts and actions. She is seeking ways to have voice in her marriage. The couple thinks their marriage has a chance.

You and I experience boundlessness within the boundaries set by God. Forgiveness and the emotional attunement of empathy it assumes open possibility, a release of revenge, deepened intimacy, and a sense of wholeness. To practice forgiveness is an act of reclamation and participation. For some, forgiveness is the beginning of a journey, for others the midpoint, and for yet others the end of a journey. A friend reminded me that forgiveness is a form of for-giveness, a gift you offer not only for yourself, but also others, especially the next generation. She also says that it is a form of for-grieving as one mourns the loss of what could have been. Forgiveness demands accountability and is never a form of cheap grace. Ultimately, it instills a sense of inner and interpersonal peace as justice is handed over to God. The Hebrew for "forgiveness," *salah*, I am reminded, is used only with respect to God's activity. *Salah* is a Godly act and knows no boundaries, for its origin is in God. We incarnate God when we forgive. By for-giving, we become co-creators with God.

Who can give the gift and the grace of forgiveness? How might forgiveness change you?

Besides forgiveness, another example of practicing boundlessness with others is partaking in a *minga*. A *minga* is a gift we receive from the South American Andes. We find it in Peru, Chile, and Ecuador, but *minga* now has emigrated to Afghanistan and the high courts of the world where decisions are made regarding the global ecological crisis. *Minga* is a Quechua word that predates Inca rule and means *coming together with others as a community for the betterment of all*. Think of the Amish barn raisings and Habitat for Humanity builds where a community creates something good in little time with all contributing. Whether the community builds a school, a community center, or a house, installs a water system, repairs a road, or maintains a forest, the whole that a *minga* creates is always bigger than the parts used in the construction or the number of people participating. The gift of a *minga* thus flows into a community, such flow being a common trait of play-fullness. Another gift of a *minga* is that it deepens the connection between an individual and the community. As you practice play-fullness with others, seeking opportunities to engage in a *minga* is a natural choice.

How can you empower yourself to partake in a *minga*? What might you gain from such an experience?

By partaking in a form of *minga,* you become a true politician, someone who is shaping a "city" or community according to values that enrich the lives of all its citizens or members. Imagine living in a neighborhood or town shaped by mutual respect and compassion!

Boundlessness requires that we discover all persons as created in the image of God. To do this, we need to do away with any preconceived notions we have of people. Living in an overtly Christian community, my family and I have reached out to friends who are Muslim, Hindu, Baha'i, and Pentecostal as persons of faith. We come from many countries. Discovering each other beyond the stereotypes we receive in the media is a definite challenge, but also a gift. After attending Friday prayer meetings with our Muslim friends, for example, my family had to admit that we do not take prayer as seriously as our friends do. And our Baha'i friends made us question the level of tolerance we have as we confess "love your neighbor as you love yourself." Learning to celebrate diversity has been the one goal that keeps us connected. When someone xenophobic in our town spray-painted racial slurs on a family's driveway, we ate a communal meal with this family to protest the injustice and to communicate our sense of solidarity. Being part of diversity is an experience of boundlessness.

How would you be enriched if you could grow beyond your fear of strangers or grow from *tolerating* diversity to *celebrating* diversity?

Practice boundlessness with others by:

- ◆ Seeking out and participating in the lives of others
- ◆ Entering into cross-cultural or interfaith friendships
- ◆ Keeping healthy boundaries toward and with others

- Seeking communal purposes and joining causes that are bigger than just your own interest
- Engaging in activities with others that suspend time, activities such as hospitality, playing games together, and engaging in a communal project
- Joining others in nature
- Experiencing diverse spiritualities within the Christian tradition

When we practice boundlessness with others, things tend to slow down, for the sense of community we create suspends time.

Practicing Slowness with Others

In chapter 3 I said that *slowness* encourages you to do things at the right speed, to savor the tastes, smells, sights, and sounds of life, to touch life gently and not to rush through time and space. Practicing slowness with others takes many forms. It includes thinking local and not global. The Stoddart family did so by joining a CSA (Community Supported Agriculture) group. The M.E.A.T. club I am a part of is an exercise both in slowness and in hospitality. We only eat food we prepare ourselves, often joining the host in the kitchen as he prepares a feast and slowly enjoying a glass of wine together. Likewise, the play-full parenting I described above is a form of slow parenting, where connection is of central importance. Slow parenting discourages what Carl Honoré calls hyperparenting, a parenting style that wants to speed our children along according to the principles of achievement, pressure, and the Fast Life. Slow parenting resists schedules governing children, offering much time for free play. Slowness also speaks to our intimate lives. Since we live in a world where sex is a Fast Life commodity, I would like to focus on slow relationships, which include slow partnering, slow intimacy, and slow sex.

In a world where 140 characters on a cell phone have become a normal form of communication, slow relationships have become less common. Fortunately for me, my aging parents in South Africa do not have a computer. I have tried for the past few years to call them daily. Now some might say that this is a form of co-dependence, but I would disagree. Since connection, whether to persons, your local area, or to the earth is central to practicing slowness, speaking to my parents daily has slowed us down. When I call, we tend to talk only about today, since tomorrow we'll speak again. The emotional connection between us has deepened considerably even though I am about twelve thousand miles removed in a different hemisphere. My mother used to be the chief communicator in their marriage. Mom would answer the phone, never Dad. And if Dad did speak to me, it was only for a few sentences before he passed the phone back to Mom. Over the years, however, Dad has grown into a person who now talks at length on the phone, and not only about the weather but also about his personal health concerns and vulnerabilities, his political views, and more.

To be in a slow relationship, one has to communicate. Of course, having communication skills is not as natural as we would like to believe. We help our partners by speaking in short sentences and not long monologues. We suspend our own opinions and leave our assumptions at the door. We receive what our partners share, valuing the gift they offer us, refraining from any urge to evaluate what they say. Receiving someone's communication is difficult, especially if the other person is upset or angry with us. Slow relationships are thus much more than saying: "I hear you" or "I understand." Actually, those statements speak to a Fast Life where quick decisions are made, empathy is nowhere to be found, and people are problems that need fixing or lifestyles that need to be controlled. Far from being passive, slow relationships are extremely active, being responsive not only to the other person, but also to your own conscious and even unconscious emotional reactivity. In slow relationships, we follow the other person or persons deeper into meaning and mystery rather than pulling or coaxing them to join us where we are. We exist for the other. Slow relationships, then, are characterized by accurately communicating empathy, respect, and genuineness, and by staying with the person or persons with whom we are conversing and not "leaving the room" by discussing persons not present to the conversation.

Deepen an existing relationship by communicating with each other often, even daily.

Slow partnering is an essential part of being play-full. God created you to be in an intimate relationship. Denying someone the gift and grace of an intimate relationship, as some churches do with persons who are gay, lesbian, bisexual, or transgendered, cries out against God as our Creator. In the introduction I said that I wrote this book to empower persons in "the Four P's of life": Personhood, Partnering, Parenting, and Profession. Partnering includes all our intimate relationships, from friendships to marriage and family. It also includes our partnership with the earth. But here I am thinking especially of our relationship with our intimate partners, our partner.

Certainly, effective communication greatly determines the quality of our partnering. But so too does love, commitment, trust, patience, kindness, humility, serenity, and perseverance. And, of course, we can add play-fullness. This love, Scripture reminds us, never fails. When play-fullness enters into our relationship with our intimate partner, we become not only one flesh, but also one spirit. We may have a relationship that is proper and polite, with promises of a good life, but it may lack play-fullness, and we never become one spirit. Such a relationship lacks realness, boundlessness, or even creativity, all of which bring excitement and newness to a relationship. In chapter 1 you met Martin and Emma who, having lost their jobs, discovered the importance of being able to receive gifts from friends. Receiving always slows us down, for it denies our agentic nature of always wanting to do things, of being the one in control. And in chapter 3 Deb and Rick deepened their relationship by being hosts to Christine, who was grieving the death of her husband.

> Since togetherness, romance, and nondemanding touch are key to slow partnering, increase these ways of being together.

Sarah and her partner, Holly, have done much work in their relationship to be more play-full. They have overcome tendencies to criticize each other, to be in competition with each other by asking who contributes more to the finances of their household, and they have moved beyond conflict with others as they try to be a lesbian couple in a heterosexual world. Sarah and Holly practice slowness by engaging in a few practices: they eat breakfast together and prepare their brown bag lunch together; then they share how they anticipate their day will go. Arriving home at night, they greet each other before they greet the dog, then they prepare a meal together, which they eat at their kitchen table. Wanting romance to be part of their relationship, they eat by candlelight and have a glass of their favorite wine. Over dinner they talk about their day, tending not to share factual information about other people so much as sharing how their inner spaces changed during the day and in what emotional state they arrived back home. They ask about the dreams each one has for their personal future and where they would like to be a few years from now. Sarah typically then watches some television while Holly spends time engaged in one of her hobbies. By 9:00 p.m. their television is shut off and they retreat to their bedroom at the same time where one often asks the other for a deep tissue massage. Touch is central to slow intimacy. Sometimes they share a bath. Sarah, a night owl, sometimes gets out of bed after Holly is asleep to read or catch up on e-mails.

The sharing of our inner lives, our dreams, passions, and fears, is central to being play-full with our partners. Without sharing those things that leave us vulnerable, we risk not introducing a core aspect of ourselves to our partners. Practicing slowness through conversation and being in each other's presence will deepen your intimate relationships.

A play-full person in a committed intimate relationship practices slow sex. Slow sex and sexual intimacy are attempts at redeeming human sexuality that has been co-opted by the Fast Life. The Fast Life turns sexuality into another commodity, something we compulsively engage in with a competitive spirit as we strive for multiple orgasms to be reached at the same time. We have sexual intercourse without much or any connection; we engage in the two-dimensional, genitalized sexuality of pornography. We make a "date" for sexual intercourse as we would make an appointment with the dentist or our physician. There is no spontaneity in the Fast Life, only planned reactivity. Slow sex recognizes that we were created as sexual beings and as such we need guidelines, a sexual ethic of sorts, which keeps us safe from the cultural force of the Fast Life as we nurture our sexual selves. These guidelines include:

- Embracing the fact that you *are* a body with certain needs, including sexual needs

- Recognizing that you are a sexual being, always, yearning for touch, connection, and deep knowing

- Acknowledging that sexual intimacy requires emotional, relational, and spiritual maturity, even self-confidence and a healthy body image

- Accepting the responsibility that is asked for by sexual intimacy, a responsibility that ranges from parenthood to the pain of disappointment to privacy

Central to slow sex is resisting the genitalization of sexuality. The genitalization of sex reduces sexuality to a penis, a vagina, a pair of breasts, a butt, or another body part. It isolates body parts from the whole person, with the person getting lost as things speed up. We see this every day on television, in advertisements, and in newsprint. Sex has been industrialized; it is a commodity to trade and sell. Slow sex denies a sexuality that is found on a screen or received by *merely* drinking alcohol to remove some anxiety and taking a pill to awaken desire. True to the Fast Life, there are more quick-fix pills available for men than for women, pills that can speed up blood flow to the penis. Do not be mistaken: play-fullness does not deny us the joy of a quickie with our intimate partner, but it will question if that is the only way sexual intimacy is experienced. Thus, as the genitalization of sex is denied, slow sex deepens the emotional, spiritual, and relational gift of sex. Furthermore, it allows our bodies, especially the female body, to become aroused.

This process begins long before we reach our bedrooms, as touch, conversations, flirting and teasing, sharing fantasies, creating ambience in the room, and, yes, much foreplay, all become part of slow sex. We limit the possibility of intrusion, whether the television or phones or children, just as we remove expectations placed on our partners, such as multiple orgasms or even orgasm at all. Rather, discover the joys locked up in our bodies, educate each other on what would be pleasurable, guide hands to sensuous areas of the body. Breathe rhythmically together. Attune to each other. Trust and give up your need for control. Listen, watch, sense, empower. Smell and taste. Enjoy the love between you and your intimate partner in an unhurried manner. End your time together cuddling or holding hands or talking some more. Hold off sleep for a while longer. Remain mindful in what you do.

We find such play-fullness in intimacy and sexuality in Solomon's Song of Songs. In this poetic book, imagination and desire enrich the love between two lovers. She says her lover is as precious as a sachet of myrrh, that he is a young stag. He says her eyes are like doves; she is a lily among thorns. She searches for him and brings him back to a special room in her mother's house. She says she has taken off her robe.... Both find delight in each other, celebrating each other's body, finding beauty in mouths, lips, teeth, eyes, temples, and more. Each one saying that they have awakened desire in the other. Slow intimacy and sexuality follow ancient paths....

Practicing slowness calls upon us to enjoy the moment, to foster deep connection, to engage in sustainable practices. These principles govern our intimate lives too.

Slow down your sexual relationship with your intimate partner. Ask your partner how that might be possible.

Seeking play-fullness, we need to find ways to slow down our intimate lives. As you can imagine, practicing slowness with others takes many additional forms:

- Eating a home-cooked meal, preferably with locally grown ingredients, around the family table or in the kitchen

- Visiting with a person who is lonely or depressed

- Joining a Community Supported Agriculture (CSA) venture, a community garden, or going fishing with a friend

- Being spontaneous with others, doing things on the spur of the moment

- Shaping your community with others around a principle such as compassion or justice

- Sharing with neighbors electrical and motorized equipment such as drills, chain saws, lawnmowers, power washers, and snow blowers

- Seeking wisdom in tradition, experience, and understanding, whether by calling upon artisans, craftsmen, or by doing something "traditional" such as line dancing or attending a Renaissance Fair

Since cooking a meal and enjoying the feast is a natural way to practice slowness with others, practicing hospitality with others is almost a given. But hospitality is so much more....

Practicing Hospitality with Others

In chapter 3 I said that the practice of hospitality creates space for others and for yourself. It has the power to transform, as Abraham and Sarah discovered when three guests became One. As we give food and water and even clothing to people, and as we visit people in some form of bondage, we follow the will of God. We are hospitable because it is a spiritual and ethical mandate. God requires it of us. And as Deb and Bob discovered as they entertained the grieving Christine, being hospitable to others enriches one's life and deepens one's relationships. I discovered the same in the M.E.A.T. club. Almost by definition, hospitality speaks more about you hosting others than anything else.

> Name three or four reasons why being hospitable toward others would be a play-full practice to embrace.

Earlier I said that to the question, "What did Jesus do?" one answer is: He walked! But following the previous chapter, where Jesus' enemies described him as a glutton and a drunkard, one might also answer this question in the following way: He would eat with people and enjoy some wine. Following Jesus is usually a good idea, even if it can cost you your life! Feasting together or being a guest at a feast is a central theme in Scripture, whether it is Psalm 23 reminding us that the table is prepared for us before our enemies, feasting on five loaves and two fishes with baskets of leftovers, or a banquet where none of those invited will feast, but instead people from the streets and country lanes are invited in. Scripture beckons us to give a feast and invite the poor, the maimed, the lame, and the blind. And to think that we tend to practice hospitality only toward friends we know well!

Imagine being a host. What feelings
and thoughts come to mind?

From Southern Africa we receive a beautiful word: *ubuntu*. Numerous African languages have a word describing this rich concept. Ubuntu speaks of community and belonging. A brief definition might be something like: "I am because we are." Ubuntu speaks to many things: community, care, belonging, and also hospitality. With an estimated 11.6 million AIDS orphans in Sub-Saharan Africa (2008) and few orphanages, orphans are taken into homes having only two or three rooms. Some families have three or even four times the number of adopted children as compared with their biological children. Hospitality is lived in situations that know poverty. These families are hosting God, for that is the power of hospitality.

Inviting persons into a space that is our own requires a sense of vulnerability and the risk of failure. As we contain the risk involved, we create a comfortable, personal, and safe place for our guests. We bring our open heart to someone, risking possible wounds, but believing that in that sacred space they will find respite and restoration. Our guests bring more than just hunger and thirst; they also bring blessing, which we receive through the mutual sharing of our lives. We listen to each other, share our stories and our lives, and experience how time is suspended. As we are physically nurtured, we also are relationally and spiritually fed. All along, we are also guests of God's grace, becoming hosts as we extend that grace to others. Then we discover that in true hospitality, the distinction between host and guest disappears.

How might your sense of self change if
you imagine that you are hosting God?

West Michigan, the area my family and I call home, might be unique. Here families are extremely open to adoption. Seeing large numbers of families where one or two members are Asian or African is normal. The deep Christian roots of this area, no doubt, play an important role in this. Families adopt children from Sudan, Ethiopia, Haiti, Vietnam, Burma, Russia, China, from within the United States, and from many other places. Few experiences might highlight hospitality to others more than adoption.

Ask an adoptive family about the
blessings they receive and the burdens
they carry.

Lyle and Didi have three children of their own. They have been adoptive and foster parents for many years, welcoming children and even young adults from Sudan and Burma to join their nuclear family of three children. Some of the children they brought into their home have graduated from college and moved on into life as adults, yet they always have a home to which to return. Lyle states, "Our home is sometimes chaotic," since it is common that at any particular time between eight and twelve people live in the home they especially bought to accommodate a large family. "But," he continues, "there is so much love and support and encouragement and vitality in our home! I am blessed." Didi states that she has had a child in diapers for ten years in a row, but that she would not exchange her life surrounded by children for anything else. Lyle, Didi, and their family practice *ubuntu.*

Not all of us have the temperament or call to become adoptive or foster parents. All of us, however, carry God's mandate to be kind to strangers, whether they come from near or afar. None of us, however, lacks the gifts and means needed to be hospitable to others. Practice hospitality with others by:

- Smiling and greeting those you come across, especially persons on the sidewalks of life; or by extending an act of kindness to someone; or by expressing gratitude to a person rendering you some service

- Getting to know your neighbors

- Inviting someone or a family for dinner, even friends of the past, maybe without scheduling it far in advance

- Blessing someone by affirming and supporting someone or through philanthropy

- Being an advocate for the marginalized and the voiceless, possibly visiting a homebound person, someone in the hospital, or someone in prison

- Keeping confidences that your friends have shared with you or accepting someone without judgment

- Prohibiting someone from consuming too much alcohol and then getting behind the wheel of a car

---

In the next conversation you have, become aware of the difference between talking *with* someone and talking *to* someone. Grow in talking *with* someone.

Willie and Drew have been partners for fifteen years. In this time, they have experienced a great deal of discrimination and have received many violent threats. Still, the injustices they experienced did not harden their hearts, but had the opposite effect on them. They practice hospitality by opening their home to gay couples and share some of their struggles and discoveries with them. They also mentor men who have come out of the closet and who struggle settling on their gay identity in a conservative town. Having done this for many years, Willie and Drew's hospitality includes companioning with friends dying of HIV/AIDS. For some, they have turned their house into a hospice and comforted their friends as they prepared themselves to go to God. Both state unequivocally that their ministry of hospitality is both a calling from God and a life-giving experience.

Practicing hospitality is a saving grace. Rahab, a prostitute, opened her house to two spies as Israel was about to enter the Promised Land. The king of Jericho heard about this and sent word to Rahab that she needed to hand over the spies. The hospitality she practiced infused her with strength and courage, so, risking her own life she hid the spies and lied about their whereabouts. Allowing the spies of Israel to escape by rope down the city walls, Rahab and all in her house were spared when the city's walls came tumbling down. As long as you and I have walls of conflict and competition, walls of criticism and consumerism in our lives, practicing hospitality with others will probably remain elusive.

Practicing Transcendence with Others

To experience transcendence is to be moved. It is always a spiritual experience, and may be religious too. In chapter 3 I said that awe and wonder will awaken a sense of transcendence in us. In moments of transcendence we are often rendered speechless, feeling small, vulnerable, yet strangely secure in who we are and what we are witnessing. Sadly, experiences of transcendence, those moments where earth and heaven are near, do not remain alive in us for very long, requiring us to seek new experiences regularly. Sometimes we do not even recognize the presence of transcendence in our lives as we speed off living the Fast Life.

The Israelites were following Moses and Aaron aimlessly in the desert. They were hungry and they grumbled. Crowds become dangerous in moments such as these. Some Israelites even wished they were dead. God then stepped in and said bread will rain down from heaven and they should collect enough for that day and every sixth day they should collect a double portion. Quail also came and covered their camp. As this happened, the glory of God appeared in a cloud. The Israelites were content, but shortly thereafter they grumbled again, this time because they were thirsty. And God surprised them with water from a rock.

Many years later, a few thousand people surrounded Jesus, and he had compassion toward them, healing their sick. Nightfall came and his disciples said he should send the people away, obviously not wanting to be hosts to such a large group of people. How shocked the disciples must have been when Jesus told them the people need not go away, rather that the disciples should feed the people. With five barley loaves and two fishes the disciples, with Jesus, fed five thousand men alone, not counting the women and children. And there were baskets full of leftovers. The next day, the disciples and others could not fathom Jesus as the Bread of Life and grumbled again. Jesus also said that whoever drinks of the Living Water would never thirst again. We remain thirsty.

> Recall a group experience where the Transcendent touched your life and you experienced joy, awe, and wonder.

To experience transcendence is "to cross over," "to exceed," or "to go beyond." Experiences of transcendence are most often temporary and difficult to put into words. Furthermore, we tend to be passive or in a receptive state in those moments, leaving the moment with a sense that we've learned something or gained something valuable. Sometimes an encounter with the Transcendent, due to its otherworldly nature, evokes a sense of fear linked with fascination. Sometimes we respond with laughter.

Someone once said that the essence of friendship is mourning, for one friend will die first. And with that death comes the invitation to experience transcendence. The cancer has taken over much of Gail's body. She is in the final days of her life and has summoned her family to surround her. Hospice caregivers are present too. Initially her daughters, sons-in-law, and grandchildren were anxious in her presence, but they soon relaxed as they shared stories about Gail's life with one another. They recalled many Christmases at her home and summers at the family cottage, and the grandchildren told of individual vacations with Nana. When Gail was too old to travel alone, she asked her grandchildren to be her chaperones on overseas tours. Tears flowed, laughter rang out, and at times, Gail seemed to smile. She was past talking, yet looked peaceful. Her pastor visited briefly each day, silently preparing for the anticipated funeral.

Earlier that day they brushed her hair, gave her a sponge bath, added some lipstick, and sprayed her with perfume. The family gathered round Gail's bed, her breathing now shallow and intermittent. It was then that someone commented on the "presence" they felt in the room. Others agreed. It was a sacred presence, tranquil and inviting. "God is holding her," someone commented. "And us," another added. "She is going home," another said. One or two family members left the room, but the rest remained. They could feel the thin veil separating this life and the next in their midst. Gail looked peaceful, held in silence and carried with love. Then someone noticed that she was no longer breathing. They called the nurse who confirmed that she could not find a pulse. "I'll never be the same," said Gail's daughter. A grandson said this was the most important moment of his life. Others quietly cried, looked at Gail in silence, or left to call family and friends.

Experiencing transcendence comes in many forms. Few experiences are as intimate as being with someone who is dying. Place yourself in a position where you can experience transcendence by:

- Joining a sacred community

- Worshiping in a cathedral

- Practicing religious rituals with others

- Attending a music concert

- Summiting a mountaintop at dawn or dusk with family or friends

- Comforting someone who is dying

In Conclusion

The polar bear moved closer and closer to the husky sled dogs tethered outside a kennel in Churchill, Manitoba. The dogs went crazy as the bear approached, but one dog, Hudson, stood his ground and began to wag his tail. Photographer Norbert Rosing, there to photograph the dogs at sunset, tells that the bear appeared out of nowhere and touched noses with the dog as if to greet. Another bear appeared and walked to another dog, rolled on his back and the bear and dog starting roughhousing. No fangs were shown nor could any signs of hostility be seen. The bear returned for the next ten days playing with the dogs, never hurting anyone. Events such as this one have also been reported between grizzlies and wolves. Even in nature a sense of play can bridge hostilities millennia old. Imagine what being play-full with others might mean for our world!

As the economic realities of people change, employment opportunities diminish, and shame and despair set in, we often read about murder-suicides in newsprint. How desperate must a person be to kill family or friends or co-workers and then themselves? Today, being play-full with others is more needed than ever. When we are play-full especially with our children, we engage in an act of generativity, an act that fosters peace and justice in the current younger generation. Whether your play-fullness with others takes you to Disney World anticipating a parade, to a football stadium surrounded by thousands of fans, or to dining with an intimate group of friends, being with others fulfills a deep need in our lives.

Unfortunately, play-fullness with others is not as natural as we imagine, so be deliberate in your play-fullness. The intentional nature of play-fullness asks of you to join with others and move into their world or invite them into yours. When you do, you will communicate interest, connection and inclusion, freedom, stability in the midst of change, and a sense of safety and security in moments of a specific fear or general anxiety.

Next we look at being play-full with God.

SIX

Being Play-full with God

What have we forgotten about God? This question came to me as I read a wonderful story. A three-year-old girl anticipated the arrival home of her newborn baby brother. Within hours of his arrival she insisted that her parents leave her alone with her new brother. She told them she wanted to spend time with him in his room with the door shut. As expected, the parents were very uneasy about a three-year-old and a three-day-old being alone together, but they reminded themselves that they do have an intercom system and can listen to what might happen. With some trepidation they granted their older child her request, allowed her to enter her brother's room, and shut the door. Listening in, they heard footsteps across the room and imagined their daughter standing next to the crib. Then they heard her saying: *"Tell me about God — I've almost forgotten."*

This evocative story reminds us that we come from God and carry a deep longing to be reconnected with our Creator. As we learn about this life, however, our forgetting increases. With the birth and growth of individuality and self-awareness we receive forgetfulness. And as the enemies of play-fullness appear in our lives, God becomes more remote. *"Tell me about God — I've almost forgotten."* Both the little girl's curiosity about God and the wisdom about her diminishing knowledge of God are traits of a play-full life.

Becoming play-full is more than just a way of living; it is also a way of believing and knowing God. As the title of this chapter indicates, we will explore being play-full with God. Whether you would describe yourself as a "Christian," an "Evangelical," a "Catholic," a "Protestant," "just spiritual" or maybe even a "doubter," being play-full with God can inform your relationship with the Divine. Such play-fullness follows naturally if being play-full when alone and with others informs your living. There are many spiritual paths one can walk and the ones that include play-fullness with God are different from the others. God longs to engage you at a deep level, seeking ways to meet you face-to-face, and such intimacy almost always awakens a sense of play-fullness in us. A play-full spiritual path inevitably leads you into community where people together are play-full with God.

Imagine the difference between *faith* and *belief in,* and live faithfully.

As a way of knowing, being play-full with God teaches us something new not only about God but also about ourselves. I believe it was the theologian Harvey Cox who suggested that thinking of oneself as someone who can imagine, hope, and play instead of seeing oneself as sinner or even merely a creature, leads to new insights. Whereas the enemies of play-fullness — conflict, control, criticism, competition, compulsion, and consumption — direct you away from God and come between you and God, play-fullness assists you in becoming godlier. It informs righteous living where peace and justice surround and guide you. I'm reminded that the literal meaning of the word "belief" in the Bible means "faithing into." "Faithing into" should not be confused with "believing in" something or Someone. To believe requires much more than an Object to believe in as you grow in the ability to be intimate with God. On this journey of growth and discovery you will discover God as the Player who played eternally before all of creation, a God who created a large playground for your enjoyment. Imagine God, playing with the leviathan — God's pet dragon — now inviting you into a play-full relationship.

Chances are good that you already practice play-fullness with God, for many of the common ways you engage God are evident through this lens. Remember, we defined play-fullness as imaginatively and creatively engaging your self, others, God, and all of reality so that peace and justice reign within you and with others. The "between" nature of play-fullness naturally takes us to "faithing into" where we are transformed after experiencing the Sacred. To be play-full is not to be irrelevant or irreverent, but rather to become increasingly aware of God's activity in your life and the sacredness shining forth from people and the created order. When something is happening in you and between you and God, you are being play-full with God. You are also play-full when you:

- Pray or talk with God
- Read the Bible, inspirational material, and spiritual autobiographies
- Sing a hymn or a spiritual song
- Worship with others
- Wonder how God is present in this world
- Contemplate the nature of God's being
- Practice rituals such as weddings and funerals
- Experience sacraments such as Holy Communion or baptism
- Ask: Why me? Or, Why God?

In which of these play-full activities do you now engage? You are already play-full with God, but I assume you are looking for ways to deepen that journey. It is grace that being play-full with God does not require you to be sacrilegious or even unorthodox. Rather, play-fullness is the invitation you receive from God, who invites you into a personal relationship with the Divine. In this final chapter, I revisit the play-full practices first described in chapters 2 and 3. Whether it is realness, creativity, or boundlessness, all the practices identified for cultivating play-fullness can be identified in the person of God.

Practicing Realness with God

Realness, you recall, challenges you to hold paradox, resist black-and-white thinking, and to view yourself as someone holding inherent tensions or polarities. Some of the tensions are that you feel alive sometimes and are bored other times, that you are vulnerable yet also cold-hearted, and that you are loving and kind even as your destructiveness lurks nearby. You have received and continue to receive realness as a gift when you are loved. This love can come from significant people in your life, partners, and family and friends, but possibly also from a dog or other pet. Of course, God loves you. Remember, your realness stems from God, in whose image you're made.

Seeing a burning bush and hearing the words, "I am who I am," Moses entered onto ground so sacred he removed his shoes. We can imagine the confusion in Moses when he had to tell the Israelites that "I am" sent me and how the Israelites received this message. God, the "I am," named, yet mysteriously unknown. Moses, recognizing the sacredness of the moment, hid his face and never saw God. The burning bush tells of a fiercely independent God, yet one who enters into a relationship with Israel and people like us. We recognize the realness of God in his name, "I am who I am," but also in God's self-portrayal as a loving, caring God, slow to anger and harboring abundant love, yet also a God who judges and destroys. We experience God's realness in God's "alongsideness," which we name God Emmanuel, God with us, and in God's "overagainstness." God is the Other who hands down the Ten Commandments and who will return in Christ to judge the living and the dead. God alongside, God overagainst. God became flesh in Jesus and when we enter into a relationship with Jesus, we have to practice realness, for Jesus is fully human, fully Divine.

When crisis befalls us and we ask "Why, God?" we are practicing realness with God. Sometimes we use the words of the Psalmist who said: "How long, O Lord? Will you forget me forever? How long will you hide your face from me?" Or, we echo "My God, my God, why have you forsaken me?" How can you believe in a God who seeks you out, who wants to be face-to-face with you, yet whose face, at times, might be hidden? And, how can you "faith into" when God's promises include blessings, but all you experience is a burden?

Andrew has been married four years and with his wife, Yolanda, is expecting their first child. He was surprised at being out of breath after mowing his lawn. The next day, walking nine holes on a golf course he was totally exhausted and could barely finish. With the encouragement of Yolanda, Andrew went to their doctor. They know something was wrong when their physician asked them to come to her office to receive the results of the blood tests. Struggling to look them in the eye, the doctor informed Andrew that he has a form of life-threatening leukemia. The news was devastating.

How have crisis situations changed the
way you experience and see God?

At first, Andrew felt he needed to be optimistic for himself and Yolanda. He spent hours on the Internet researching his illness and reading blogs of persons who had a similar diagnosis. Some of those people died. As his focus on life shifted to his illness, however, all kinds of questions came to him: Why me? Why God? Why now? Why would God allow this to happen, so close to the birth of their first child? If God did not "cause" the cancer, who did? Sometimes he wondered whether God was punishing him for being sexually active as a teenager or some other sin he committed. Then he thought that this disease might be God's will for his life, or that

God wants to send a message to him through the cancer. Other times he contemplated how God is present in his life, even now. To those who asked, he described his life and his marriage as being on a spiritual roller coaster.

As his journey continued, Andrew prayed a simple prayer of lament. To lament is to be play-full with God, for it engages God in a form of communication that acknowledges the limitation of an embodied life. Lament grants permission to mourn and protest yet transcends the current moment and reality by instilling hope. Ultimately, lament prepares us to experience God and others anew, since it removes cynicism and apathy, purifies anger, and diminishes a desire for vengeance. Andrew prayed:

> Dear God, please hear my prayer. You have done so in the past. The doctors tell me the cancer is bad. The chemotherapy is ravaging my body just as the cancer is doing. I am afraid that I may not see my unborn child. I'm afraid of what the cancer might do. I do not want to die and leave Yolanda to raise our child alone. Lord, thank you that you know my fears. I believe that every day you are with Yolanda and our baby, with my physicians, and with me. Spirit of God, I pray that your healing touch will rest upon me. Grant me the gift of health and help me to notice your presence in my life. Thank you for receiving this prayer, O God. In Jesus' name I pray. Amen.

Praying this lament and others similar to it, Andrew felt a sense of peace that truly transcended his circumstances. His mind-set further changed when a friend asked him why he ascribes his cancer to God and not to life in general. Thinking about that some more, Andrew felt a sense of peace coming over him as he thought of God being with him, even now. His prayer changed from one that seeks healing to one that asks God to help him notice God's presence in his life. One day he realized that the why questions no longer occupied his mind. He recognized that he always saw God as a Being that created goodness in and for people. Now he saw

God as a Presence inviting him into a relationship, in whatever life situation he is in. Andrew continued his chemotherapy, holding the tension between a God who is all-powerful and yet a God who does not work miracles with every prayer. A God who responds to every request with a miracle, Andrew decided, would be a handy idol. Andrew's oncologists are optimistic about his future, and together with Yolanda, Andrew is picking out names for their baby.

Think of a loss or concern you carry and pray a simple lament:

+ Call on God

+ Name your complaint

+ Express faith that God heard your complaint

+ Petition God

+ Express faith that God heard your petition

+ Praise God and express gratitude

Practice realness with God by:

+ Holding the tension between God's "alongsideness" and God's "overagainstness"

+ Praying a lament

+ Finding meaning in life's circumstances

+ Discovering God in new ways

+ Refusing to turn God into an idol

+ Allowing nature to teach you about the Sacred

+ Contemplating God as a Mystery

To practice realness with God is to discover God anew. Jewish philosopher Martin Buber wrote that one can have either I/It relationships or I/Thou relationships. An I/It relationship signifies a monologue between a subject and an object, whereas an I/Thou relationship represents a dialogue between two subjects. An I/Thou relationship portrays a sense of honesty and rawness, for the relationship is not necessarily mediated by something else, such as a belief system. Growing toward I/Thou relationships, one discovers another person or group without holding on to preconceived notions and refusing to relate to only one part of a person as is found in I/It relationships. Buber observed that the more one analyzes someone, the more one turns that person into an It, an object known outside of any relationship. By accepting the divinity and uniqueness of God's "alongsideness" and "over-againstness," for example, we discover God as the Eternal Thou. God becomes real for us. This practice of holding the tensions within God's being, as one does in praying a prayer of lament, is a way of practicing creativity with God.

Practicing Creativity with God

Adam, at the very beginning of our history, initiated the practice of co-creativity with God. With creation spoken into existence by God just before Adam received his partner, God brought all the creatures to Adam so that he could name them. To name someone, an animal or plant, especially in Old Testament times, is a powerful symbolic act. We tend to protect, guard, and be stewards of the natural world, or we claim dominion over the created order, which in turn leads to exploitation and ultimately ruin. The language we use constructs our reality, and naming is part of that reality, for in naming we determine the worth of something. You discovered the power of naming realities if you engaged the experiment in chapter 3 by telling yourself, "My life is really busy right now" one day and, "It's a wonderful day filled with possibility" the next. If you add a third day saying: "God wants to tell me something, so I am keeping my eyes and ears open," I imagine God will speak to you many times during the day.

To be play-full in your relationship with God is to risk not mentioning God's name at all and to find new ways of addressing God. St. Francis of Assisi said that no one is worthy to pronounce God's name. Likewise the prophet Jeremiah said, "I will not mention him or speak any more in his name" (Jer. 20:9). Not mentioning God's name is not a prohibition but rather an invitation to discover the mystery of the One who was, the One who is, and the One who will come again. To be creative in your relationship with God is to know God beyond a Name, even beyond language. It is recognizing that the Infinite cannot be captured by the finite.

One way of practicing creativity with God is to reflect on the multiple names given to God in Scripture, for each of these names can inform your life in unique ways. How would the following names and images of God speak into your spirituality?

The God who Sees	(El Roi)
The Self-existent One	(Yahweh; "I am who I am")
The Lord who Provides	(Jehovah Jireh)
The Lord who Heals	(Jehovah Rophe)
The Lord who Sanctifies	(Jehovah Maccaddeshcem)
The Lord of Peace	(Jehovah Shalom)
The Lord our Righteousness	(Elohim Tsidkenu)
Creator	
Potter	
God as Mother Hen	
Jesus as a Vine	
The Spirit as a Flame	
Comforter	
The Beginning	(Alpha)
The End	(Omega)

If we know God only in the typically dominant terms of Father, Son, and Holy Spirit, we constrain ourselves greatly in terms of discovering God anew and deepening our relationship with the Divine. As a play-full person, ask yourself: How have I discovered God in new ways recently? Or, Where have I noticed the work of God this past week? As we deepen our relationship with God, we discover much about God and ourselves. The names of God teach us about God's nature and expose our true being. Every trait of God is also a trait we carry. We see a loved one or someone who suffers, for example. We *reach out* with love to our child and see his or her face lit up. We *nurture peace* in our inner space, in our interpersonal relationships, and in the world. We *touch* our intimate partner and feel the warmth between us.

What might God be seeing in your life? In what ways does God provide? How are you shaped and reshaped by the Potter? What sorrows do you have that the Comforter can carry for you?

Besides being play-full by addressing God in various ways, extending love, grace, and compassion to others is arguably the best way to practice creativity with God. Love is a creative force that promises realness, patience, kindness, and goodness. Love also keeps us from wandering down angry, vengeful, or envious paths.

Jim practices creativity with God. A cook serving guests at a community center, Jim has seen the number of guests he serves increase as the economy dwindled. Five days a week, Jim and his volunteers feed hundreds of people. Area grocery stores send him their food items nearing an expiration date. In summer, local farmers drop off some of their squash, corn, and tomatoes. Using the donated food and adding some he purchases, Jim creates tasty meals. Many guests say the best part is the dessert, but others say it is the love, respect, and dignity they receive from Jim and his volunteers — courtesies not always given them as people looking for jobs, struggling with addiction, or finding themselves homeless. When we practice creativity with God, people are not only fed, they feel loved. Food becomes a feast.

Whereas Jim identifies with being a host, Monica identifies with Jesus as a servant washing feet. She does this literally. Monica visits elderly people in retirement homes and offers them free pedicures. She states that at first people were a little self-conscious when she offered to wash their feet, clip their toenails, and rub oil into their feet. But word quickly spread and now people sign up for her gift of care and love. Monica creatively interprets Jesus, who washed the feet of his disciples. Her own life is enriched, she states, for she imagines that washing the feet of a stranger is the same as washing the feet of Jesus. A few close friendships have developed between her and her new sisters and brothers — after all, washing feet is a very intimate act.

John, a pastor, practices a different kind of creativity with God. With play-fullness he prays "picture prayers." John takes an image from Scripture, such as Jesus being baptized, and then imagines himself into that scene. He becomes Jesus, thinking of the significance of God telling him he is a beloved child, someone who makes God proud. Then he imagines the Spirit as a wild and free dove settling on him, empowering him to do things he cannot do by himself. And then there are the bystanders, people observing all that is happening, and John wonders how they would describe what is happening. These picture prayers, John states, are comforting and strengthening at the same time.

Imagine you are at a feast prepared for you by God, as the Psalmist writes. How do you imagine this feast? What conversations would you have with your Host, the Living God? How might your life look different when you leave this table? Practicing creativity with God as Host, for example, opens possibilities that envisioning God as a Potter cannot do. Now, if God shaped you as a Potter, and therefore has the ability to reshape you as you take form, how would others recognize God's imprint on your person?

Practice creativity with God by:

+ Addressing God by many names

+ Serving others

+ Praying in pictures

+ Extending God's love to someone

+ Becoming a Good Samaritan to someone

+ Caring for the environment

+ Receiving the kindness and compliments of others

When you practice creativity with God, you become an ambassador of sorts, not only representing God, but also offering to others some of the gifts of love, care, and compassion with which God has entrusted you.

Practicing Boundlessness with God

What happened was so out of the ordinary that it made news headlines. Someone at a drive-through restaurant paid for the person in the vehicle behind her, and when that person arrived at the payment window, he discovered that his coffee had been paid for. Feeling obligated to extend the same gift to someone else, he "paid it backward" and soon the practice of "paying backward" became a countrywide habit. When you practice boundlessness with God, the same ripple effect takes place, for God is never constrained by boundaries and limits and does not engage life through the lens of shortage. I stated in chapter 2, we believe in a God without Borders. You already sensed God's boundlessness in Jim, who feeds a few hundred people a week. You noticed it in Elisha's widow whose oil reached her whole community, most of them probably not even aware that God was the source of that goodness. You felt it after reading about the African violet queen. Of course, you recognized the boundlessness of God in Jesus who fed many with five loaves and two fish.

How do you envision practicing boundlessness with God?

One of the boundless traits of God is God's nonviolence. We are well acquainted with the God who judges and who obliterates nations. However, there are just as many images of God being nonviolent in Scripture. Remember the king of Israel who wanted to kill his enemies, and God ordering through the prophet Elisha to feed them instead (chapter 1)? Then there are Daniel's friends, Shadrach, Meshach, and Abednego, who refused to bow to the idol, created by king Nebuchadnezzar. The story tells that Nebuchadnezzar made a golden idol and ordered everyone to worship the idol or risk death. Shadrach, Meshach, and Abednego refused to pray to the god and Nebuchadnezzar became furious with them. He ordered that a furnace be heated up seven times hotter than usual, and gave Daniel's friends one more chance. *"We do not need to defend ourselves before you in this matter,"* they answered Nebuchadnezzar. Facing death, the friends took a nonviolent stance. Enraged, the king ordered the friends to be thrown into the furnace, the heat killing the soldiers who did so. Then an angel appeared with the friends in the furnace, and they remained unscathed. Amazed at what he saw, Nebuchadnezzar praised God. "We do not need to defend ourselves," they said. Nonviolence brings not only peace, but it opens possibility for transformation. Nebuchadnezzar was transformed from a self-centered, angry, and power-hungry man into a person who said: "Praise be to the God of Shadrach, Meshach, and Abednego."

Loving your enemies, as Jesus urges his followers, speaks to the boundlessness of God. We join Jesus in bringing peace when we too become nonviolent in our thoughts, language, and behavior. We have beautiful examples in persons such as Archbishop Oscar Romero of El Salvador, Martin Luther King Jr., Rosa Parks, Dorothy Day, Mother Teresa in Kolkata (India), and Bishop Desmond Tutu in South Africa. We recognize similar nonviolence in persons such as Mahatma Gandhi, Nelson Mandela, and the Dalai Lama. Their boundless lives of forgiveness, reconciliation, and nonviolence transform lives, communities, and systems. A force in itself, nonviolence always becomes a threat to those who seek earthly kingdoms.

Of course, few of us will identify ourselves as a Bishop Tutu or a Rosa Parks. The boundlessness within nonviolence, however, is something each one of us can demonstrate:

- Ann teaches individuals and communities how to use their words to connect and not wound. She visits prisons, where she helps the wardens and the prisoners communicate more effectively. Ann also teaches pastors to foster empathic relationships with those they serve.

- Bill stands on a street corner most Thursday afternoons protesting the loss of lives in war zones, urging more peaceful approaches to solve conflict. On Wednesdays and Sundays he engages in interfaith dialogue.

- Kim seeks ways to connect persons from different cultures and religious traditions, breaking down previous misconceptions, educating, and calling forth peaceful co-existence.

- Robert has opened a medical clinic in Honduras and leads groups of medical practitioners and other volunteers to restore eyesight, repair cleft palates, and offer dental care and vaccinations. Pharmaceutical companies and hospitals donate equipment and medicine.

- Michelle designs apparel that communicates the values of peace and nonviolence. She uses organic material and ensures that those who manufactured the apparel were paid a fair wage. The screen-printing on the apparel and the packaging she uses are environmentally friendly.

- Michael works with the people who remember the abuse they received suffering under political and ethnic violence. His own hands, blown away when he received a letter bomb from South Africa's Apartheid government, reach out, hold tenderly, and give hope.

These folks are ordinary people just like you who I've been privileged to meet on my journey of life. How do you partake in the boundlessness of God? Maybe an image from the biblical book of Joel can help you find an answer. The book begins by describing a landscape devoured by locusts. Nothing is left, we read. The people lament their situation. God hears their cries and sees their devastation and promises restoration. God's Spirit is poured out on all people, young and old, male and female. Then an amazing thing happens. Water begins to flow from the throne of God and waters a valley of acacias. We are that water, flowing in infinite ways to a world in need of restoration, a world devoured by locusts such as families disintegrating and persons facing life-threatening illnesses. We flow to communities experiencing poverty, famine, and war.

Who in your immediate environment is in need of God's boundless love and grace? How do you become life-giving water to that person or group?

We are reminded of the prophet Ezekiel, who saw a river flowing from God's throne that was so wide and deep he could not cross it. On the banks of the river stood trees that bore fruit all year long. And we recall the angel who, in the New Jerusalem, showed the apostle John the river of life, as clear as crystal, flowing from the throne of God and of the Lamb. The river flowed down the middle of the great street of the city. Trees grew on its banks with vigor, giving fruit each month, their leaves used for healing. We — you — are that river. Practice boundlessness with God by:

- Remaining engaged in life
- Flowing, like water, to persons and communities in need
- Feeding the hungry and clothing the naked
- Becoming aware of the Holy
- Receiving and giving forgiveness
- Loving your enemies

Water that does not flow pools together and a dam is formed. It covers vast areas of land in a wasteland of water and mud. Likewise, we can become stagnant. On the other hand, when water becomes a flash flood, it brings devastation and erosion and does not nurture. We can judge and condemn. Water, at its best, should flow slowly, like soft penetrating rain. When we become water to others, we are not far from practicing slowness with God.

Practicing Slowness with God

You'll remember that *slowness* encourages you to do things at the right speed, to savor the tastes, smells, sights, and sounds of life, to touch life gently and not to rush through time and space. Practicing slowness with God is about seeking ways to spend more time with God. It is finding ways to deepen your experience and knowledge of God. Slowness with God also invites us to meditate on God's Word and presence in our lives. As you read in chapter 4, practicing slowness always anticipates increased communication. You dialogue with your inner critic and talk with others, deepening some relationships and establishing others. Conversing with God is central to being play-full. Imagine prayer, not as a monologue with requests, but as a dialogue between you and God. Such prayers are rarely rushed. As Steven, a good friend of mine, is fond of saying, "We need to live life at the speed of prayer."

Prayer is a form of holy listening. We tune our souls to God and listen carefully to what God's Spirit communicates to us. Most often, I believe, this message reminds us that God loves us so much that he took on our flesh and dwelt among us; that God is with us, literally living in us as the Spirit. Prayer, however, might not be as natural as we think it is. Jesus' disciples asked him: "Lord, teach us to pray, just as John taught his disciples...." Maybe we need to ask that question too. Jesus said we need not always pray publicly, but we can do so in private, for God knows our deepest longings and desires. He continued by saying that prayer does not require many or repetitive words and offered us an example:

Our Father in heaven, hallowed be your name, your kingdom come, your will be done on earth as it is in heaven. Give us today our daily bread. Forgive us our debts, as we also have forgiven our debtors. And lead us not into temptation, but deliver us from evil. Amen.

What would your life look like if you
lived your life at the speed of prayer?

Prayer is a conversation with God. In prayer, we recognize God as we enter into God's presence. We praise God for all of creation and for the salvation we received. We thank God for the gift of life and for mercies received, mercies such as love, peace, faith, redemption, family and friends. In prayer we confess the fact that we do not love our neighbor as we love ourselves. To do this, of course, we have to be mindful where our hostility and even hatred touched our own lives or someone else's life. We petition God as we express deep-felt needs or ask for wisdom. We intercede on behalf of others in need of God's grace and presence by praying for specific needs of which we are aware. If we do not know specific needs, we ask our friends or the persons for whom we pray. Also, in prayer we listen to what God might be telling or showing us. Practicing slowness with God through prayer, we pray often, through the life we live, knowing that how we come to God — with an attitude of humility and reverence — is always more important than what we say or even how we say it. Prayer, always, is not about words per se, but about our relationship with God. Relationship matters, even if it is a newly established relationship. Our "best" prayers might be the ones we pray with the heart of a child: simple, short, specific, and filled with trust and anticipation.

> Draft a prayer list and then dialogue with God daily, possibly beginning with the prayer that Jesus taught his disciples.

One of the ways Shannon practices slowness with God is to meditate on a text for a period of time and allowing that text to speak to him. Finding himself in an anxious situation, Shannon returned to a parable he had resonated with since childhood. It is the parable of the Good Samaritan, a story where a man, beaten by robbers, is helped in person and financially by a person socially frowned upon, while two different kinds of church folk skirt past the helpless man, casting a blind eye. After a week of reading the story in Luke every morning and evening and thinking about the story often during the day, Shannon wrote in his journal:

This is day seven of walking with the Good Samaritan. Many thoughts have come to me: "When I'm beat up, I can allow people to help me"; "It's okay to be a victim"; and, "People who are truly my neighbor will help me." Wednesday I thought: "Difficult circumstances can arise quickly and without warning. My true community can help." Soon, that thought was replaced by: "Some people don't care about me and my needs." I ended thinking "God doesn't always protect us in this life" and "Grace comes from sometimes unexpected people." I had some other thoughts too, but these are the big ones. Never would I have guessed that one story I knew so well could speak to me on so many levels. There are possibilities in these thoughts. I wonder how God is going to use this in my life.

As persons of faith, we are persons of the Word. The Psalmist says that God's Word is a lamp to our feet, a light for our path. Sadly, we know less of God's Word than previous generations. Even self-identified Christians do not seem to read God's Word. Your journey of becoming play-full with God will be diminished if you do not engage Scripture and other sacred texts on a regular basis. Reading the Bible in community can deepen your experience, for you will discover that there are many ways to understand Scripture. Committing time during the week to engage in prayer and read Scripture or spiritual autobiographies highlights a third way to practice slowness with God: keeping *Sabbath*.

Sabbath is about a day of rest, where the work we do is celebration and contemplation. Keeping Sabbath is acknowledging that we cannot sustain ourselves by work alone and that a day (or even a portion of the day) of slowing down is beneficial for self and soul. A play-full life is essentially a contemplative life, a life often seen in the past as superior to a life of action. Sabbath and contemplation envoke images of being reflective, calm, receptive, still, unhurried or patient, and seeking quality over quantity. *The spirit in us is slow, even when it quickens.* It always seeks connection with self, others, God, and nature. The Psalmist succinctly states: "Be still, and know that I am God."

Sabbath is a day on which we do things differently. It is not so much a day that we take off or a day we rest, but a day we deliberately approach with different values and goals and relationships in mind. On every day of the week we can shop and run errands. On the day we take Sabbath time we slow down, cease our busy-ness and business, for contemplation on a full life requires mindfulness. In our consumer-driven culture, committing to a Sabbath time is an act of courage, of purposely altering our rhythm. The promise of Sabbath is that it revitalizes body, mind, and soul. You reclaim your self and soul, your home, your money, your environment, in short, your life.

Find mini-moments of Sabbath time every day and commit to a longer period of contemplation once a week.

Practicing slowness with God takes us beyond a given day of the week that we set aside for contemplation into a larger season such as Lent, that period of forty days in which we walk with Jesus to his crucifixion. *Lent is a slow time.* Some people pray, others fast, and others forego a privilege. The journey of the cross comes at a cost that should be reckoned and not rushed. If you contemplate the journey that Jesus was on, stopping at key moments on his journey such as where he is given his cross, where he falls for the first time under the weight of the cross, where he is stripped of his garments and nailed to the cross, and where he dies, the forty days of Lent are long days. Practice slowness with God by:

- Praying often
- Journaling your relationship with God
- Spending time in the sacred Scriptures
- Keeping Sabbath
- Walking a labyrinth
- Reading spiritual autobiographies
- Contemplating in nature

Samuel, the last judge to govern Israel before they asked God for a king, was yet a boy when one night he heard someone calling.

At first he thought it was his master, Eli, who was calling him, but Eli recognized that it might be God's voice Samuel was hearing. Samuel returned to his room, lay down, and waited for God. Again he heard: "Samuel! Samuel!" and finally he recognized what was happening.

Open yourself to the possibility of hearing God's voice. When you practice slowness with God, you inevitably put yourself in a position where this can happen. The voice of God is a welcoming voice, even if at times it might be a convicting voice, urging you to be more play-full and to practice slowness, or to be less judgmental of others and love your neighbor as yourself, for example. Listening, you will hear God inviting you to deepen your relationship with the One you know as Earth Maker, Pain Bearer, and Life Giver. This God is an inviting God, preparing a feast for you and all God's children.

Practicing Hospitality with God

Practicing hospitality with God is not so much something we do as it is something which we receive and into which we are invited. The Psalmist states: "Surely goodness and love will follow me all the days of my life, and I will dwell in the house of the Lord forever." And, "How lovely is your dwelling place, O Lord Almighty!" Later Jesus said: "In my Father's house are many rooms....I am going there to prepare a place for you." God is a hospitable God, a God who invites people not only to stay in a house with many rooms, but also to enter an open tomb and notice burial cloths lying around.

> In which of God's many rooms would you make your permanent dwelling?

It is nearly impossible to practice hospitality with God and not think about going to church and worshiping God in God's house.

Of course, we do not believe that God lives in a church building, but going to church creates space for us where we meet God. Worshiping God alone or with others is one way to practice hospitality as a play-full person. As we sing together and reflect on God's Word, we commune with God and are invited to leave our troubles and concerns in front of God's throne, the same throne from which life-giving water flows. This is true also for persons who walk into an empty cathedral or chapel to commune with God, lighting a candle as they enter. We practice hospitality with God when we gather with even just one or two other people to worship God or when we enter into a large sanctuary.

When we commune with God in a worship setting, two moments signify practicing hospitality with God in significant ways. The first is confessing our sinful nature and dependence upon God, and the second is being at a table as a guest. Most of us live rather independent lives. Play-full persons, however, recognize that we are never independent, but live *relatively independent* lives as we need other people to survive and thrive and as we receive life as a gift from God. When we receive God's hospitality, whether in person while in nature or meditating in silence or in a worship service, we admit our *absolute dependence* before God. By confessing our sinful nature, the fact that the enemies of play-fullness — *criticism, control, compulsion, competition, conflict,* and *consumption* — bring a rift between our neighbor and us and between God and us, expresses our need for God's forgiveness and salvation. These moments of confession are probably the only moments of the week where we find ourselves absolutely dependent upon God or anyone else.

To be absolutely dependent upon God is a position we can hold indefinitely only as a belief, but not in reality. Thus we confess our sinful nature and return to our relatively independent lives, or in moments of delusion, we believe we are independent again. However, our spirits are in need of this expression of absolute dependence for it represents more closely our true nature and reality. We come from God and carry a deep longing to be reconnected with our Creator. Furthermore, we are totally dependent on so many things we take for granted, from breathing air to drinking water. Along the way we have identified "rights" we greedily claim and forget it was gifts we received.

This week commit to enter a space where you can experience and express absolute dependence upon God. Maybe confess your sinfulness and need for redemption and a Savior.

Confessing our sinful nature and expressing our absolute dependence upon God are two related ways to practice hospitality with God. Another way is to rediscover God as the Lord of Hosts, for God invites everyone to the feast.

My family and I belong to a community that serves Holy Communion every Sunday. We stand in a circle and pass home-baked bread from person to person, saying: "This is the body of Christ, broken for you. . . . " A cup of wine follows and we remember that Christ's blood was shed for us. My daughters always break off large pieces of bread and continue eating long after everyone has finished. They eat slowly, unashamed by the breadcrumbs that surround their feet. Initially my wife and I were embarrassed since we, like others, had broken off small pieces of bread and salvaged crumbs that had made their way to the floor. Further reflection about our daughters' practice of enjoying chunks of bread showed us our limited understanding of the Lord of Hosts. Most of us are enjoying God's hospitality, but in reality we tend to confine ourselves to tiny portions of it and then spiritualize God's abundance for us. We believe that abundance is possible, but we rarely, if ever, experience it. Partaking in a communion meal is always the invitation to eat well, even as it is also an invitation to remember well. We remember the birth, life, death, and resurrection of Christ. With this meal, as with all meals the Lord of Hosts provides, everyone is welcome and the food never runs out.

What rituals do you have that link the food you eat to God?

A meal with the Lord of Hosts need not always be in a church. Any regular family meal can be enjoyed with slowness, contemplation, and a deep awareness that the food you are eating comes as a gift from God. Eating with people we care about and eating out of doors helps us to experience God's presence. So too can patiently waiting for a meal and savoring the tastes and smells, putting down your utensils between bites, and resisting eating on the run. Praying a simple prayer is often the ritual of recognizing God as Host:

> God, you open your hand and we are fed.
> Be at this table, we pray,
> and bless this, our daily bread. Amen.

Practice hospitality with God by:

+ Discovering the spaciousness of God

+ Communing in nature

+ Confessing your sinful nature and need of redemption

+ Engaging a community of faith

+ Partaking in communion

+ Rediscovering ritual as sacred play

Through the prophet Isaiah, God said: "Come, all you who are thirsty, come to the waters; and you who have no money, come, buy and eat! Come, buy wine and milk without money and without cost." God continued, saying: "My thoughts are not your thoughts, neither are your ways my ways." God transcends our reality.

Practicing Transcendence with God

In chapter 3 I said that practicing transcendence is the practice of awe and wonder. It is to be moved and to recognize that God is speaking into your daily life. As such, it is more about "this worldliness" than "other worldliness." Since being attuned to God opens you to hear God's voice or see God's presence more readily, practices such as slowness and hospitality are important. I imagine that having read this far into the book, you have practiced transcendence with God or were reminded of a time you did so.

Transcendence literally means "to climb across," and practicing transcendence with God invites you to move beyond your own self (and subjectivity) and also beyond our reality. As you climb across and move beyond, you recognize God as the Most High, exalted above the earth, as the Psalmist writes. Transcendence thus does not imply a relationship with God far away but rather speaks to discover God as the Immanent Transcendent in the space between you and God. In this space normal rules are suspended. God becomes an intimate presence as God catches your tears in a bottle and prepares a meal for you. Yet God remains totally Otherworldly, a Mystery. It is only in the potential space between you and God that the Immanent Transcendent is found. In this space, you need not deify yourself or others, nor do you need to humanize God or even minimize your sinful and destructive tendencies that lean toward the enemies of play-fullness. Rather, practicing transcendence with God is an invitation to discover self and others and God anew.

Practice transcendence with God by *surrendering* to God as the Known Mystery. Surrendering is different from submitting. One can submit to God out of fear of judgment or by negating one's

sense of self and handing that responsibility to God. Jesus, however, tells us that he calls us friends and not servants. Friends, Jesus
implied, know each other well, even if one friend can ask another
to do something. Servants, he said, do not know what their master
thinks or plans. As friends, Jesus concluded, we know what God
has in store for us, a life restored and redeemed, a full life. To
surrender is to yield, to know that engaging God changes the way
you feel and think about yourself, others, and God. Surrendering
is the appropriate response of a life of gratitude. It is to know your
past and to look forward to your future with God. Surrendering
is to let go of any notions of independence and ultimately to pro-
claim your total dependence upon God. It is giving your self up
to God. As you can imagine, a life lived out of submission and
fear is different from a life lived out of a covenant relationship of
surrendering, mutuality, and gratitude.

What would your life look like if you
were to surrender to God?

Besides surrendering to God, practice transcendence with God
by expressing *gratitude*. My octogenarian mother, Maria, is a grateful person. A person of deep, childlike faith, she has a keen sense
of awe, wonder, and gratitude, the rubrics of practicing transcendence. Since I moved to the United States, I see her less often,
but we speak almost daily by phone. Many years ago she opted
against email as a form of communication. Somewhat frustrated at
first with her choice, I am now grateful for her wisdom, for speaking with her is much more life-giving than any email I compose.
To my standard opening tongue-in-cheek question: "How are the
old folk doing?" my mother will express gratitude. Most often it
is for small things, such as a little bit of rain or a new brood of
guinea fowl in her garden. Other times it is for bigger things, such
as health for her and Barry, my father. Almost always she will

say: "Die Vader is goed vir ons" (The Father is good to us). My mother's sense of gratitude is probably as old as she is, since she has served others her whole life. For her, God is intimate, present, caring, yet a God worthy of reverence. She listens to God and hears God's voice in the rain, in the click of guinea fowl chicks, and sees it in blades of grass that turn green after 'n *katspoegie reën* (a spittle of rain). To practice transcendence with God is a practice of mindfulness. Mindfulness often leads to the expression of gratitude for a God who sees you, a God whose face is turned toward you. Your face cannot help but smile with gratitude.

Take any "spiritual" word, "faith," for example, and use it as a life-affirming acronym for:

F = *Friend*

A = *Awe*

I = *Insight*

T = *Transformation*

H = *Harmony*

Meditate on the meaning of the acronym and consciously live into that meaning. Tomorrow, and every day, take a new word: "Miracle," "Truth," "Worship," "Thou," "Forgiveness," "Sacred," "Sabbath" . . .

Whether you surrender to God or express gratitude, practicing transcendence with God is about recognizing God's *holiness* in your life and in our world. You may know this holiness since parents and pastors and others have told you that God is holy, but they may have neglected to tell you that all of creation is holy too. Feeling and recognizing God's holiness, however, speaks to a much deeper encounter with the Divine than simply *knowing* God is holy. Minnesotan artist Peter Mayer beautifully describes practicing transcendence with God in a song called "Holy Now." In the song Mayer writes how, as a child, he would go to church, where the Word and bread were holy, and where miracles, such as Moses splitting the sea in two and Jesus turning water into wine, happened in the far distant past. Now, Mayer sings, he finds holiness everywhere and the challenge is *not* seeing miracles, for they are so abundant. He walks, Mayer says, with a reverent air. A questioning child's face becomes a testament, a new morning becomes a sacrament, and the wings of a redwing black bird shine like a burning bush and speak like a scripture verse. Everything, Mayer says at the end of his song, is holy now.

> Notice holiness and witness a miracle,
> today and every day.

Practice transcendence with God by:

- Recognizing your smallness and insignificance
- Receiving God's grace
- Meditating on God as a known mystery
- Being in worship
- Hoping in the future
- Seeing a miracle unfolding
- Dying with God

Being play-full with God recognizes that you are called to live life to the full and to do so not as someone moving between relative independence and absolute dependence. God, after all, offers us a life that is rooted and redeemed, a life that experiences peace even as it pursues justice for all. On our own we can never create such a life for ourselves. We are called friends even if we have forgotten some things about God, as the three-year-old opening this chapter confessed.

In Conclusion

"Isn't being play-full with God blasphemous?" With these words my friend questioned me when I told her about this chapter. I was somewhat taken aback as she reminded me of Bible verses that discourage laughter and frivolity because they lead to mourning; also verses that warn against childishness and encouraged maturity. I reminded her that to be play-full is to engage oneself, others, and God at a significant level, that one deepens the connections one has. Being godly, I said, may be impossible without being play-full. After all, Jesus did say a life to the full is a promise given us and we know a life devoid of play is a diminished life. I cannot imagine, I said, that God spends much time making a distinction between play-fullness and seriousness. I could have shared more about how the images we have of God's *shalom*, God's reign of peace and justice, include visions of play, but we started talking about our children and the challenges of parenting. I do appreciate how many conversations seem to drift back to the essence of a play-full life, the relationships and intimate connections we keep, even if we do not consciously choose to engage our play-full lives.

Being play-full with God anticipates a meeting between you and God, and in this meeting God invites you into a covenant relationship. God comes alongside you and comforts and supports you, even carries you when your legs and spirit fail you. And God will come over against you to hold you accountable as a steward of all the gifts you have received. Some may find this kind of relationship suffocating. Many, however, have discovered that the freedom and grace we receive when we are play-full with God is essential to living a life of spontaneous responsiveness. The reactivity in which we often engage and which we see in the world is emotionally, relationally, and spiritually draining and leads to endless repetitions.

The play of God gave us creation and being and continues as the Spirit blows like the wind, its origin unknown. It is a play for its own sake. When you practice play-fullness with God, you too will experience play-fullness for its own sake. We are not play-full with God to be saved, as if salvation is the prize. No, being play-full with God is an appropriate response to the Sacred, maybe the only response worthy of God, for when we are play-full with God, categories like belief and unbelief lose all meaning.

Conclusion

What then is the right way of living? This is the question the Dutch cultural historian Johan Huizinga asked in 1938 in his book, *Homo Ludens* (Humankind at Play). The terse answer he gave was: *Life must be lived as play.* A play-full life encourages you to participate in life authentically and freely and to do so by practicing Realness, Boundlessness, Slowness, Creativity, Hospitality, and Transcendence. It is my prayer that somewhere in these pages you experienced moments of coming alive, moments where your imagination gave you glimpses of possibility, and moments where you engaged yourself and others in new ways. In those moments you experienced the power of living creatively. For that to have happened, you had to be *disloyal* to parental, cultural, and religious teachings that discourage a sense of play and that place play over against work, often judging play suspiciously and with a strict moral sense.

Even today, play is often seen as the lowest of pleasures, a danger to the Christian life in that it leads to idleness, the unproductive use of time, vanity, and sinful activities. In a world of dwindling job opportunities a (Protestant) work ethic remains elevated as a virtue. Play-fullness, however, is always good news, especially if you are burdened by a work ethic that serves such enemies of play-fullness as consumption, competition, and control. To grow in being play-full is a sure way to glorify God, and as you've discovered, being play-full is anything but idle. Without commitment and intentionality, the enemies of play-fullness, including apathy, boredom, and despondency, will determine your inner and outer experience.

Origins are important. A play-full life originates in God, who created us with the capacity for play, and in Jesus, who offers us life to the full. The word "play" stems from the Anglo-Saxon word *plegan* (or *pflegan*), a word that meant not only play, but also "plight" or "pledge." To become play-full is about making a commitment, seeing it as duty, having all intention, and keeping to a pledge. A play-full life is also something we need to educate ourselves in. It is ironic that the ancient Greeks used the same word for play as for education, *paideia* (or *paitheia*). A play-full life is truly a smart choice, one can argue, for through play-fullness, you stimulate your mind, body, and soul.

If you feel inspired to be more play-full through reading this book, then the book has lived up to its title. Through it, I have encouraged you to live a play-full life, to create a reality for yourself and others that counters many of the societal forces that render you tired, stressed, and emotionally, relationally, and spiritually depleted. Writing your own subtitle to your play-full life is an exciting challenge that awaits you. Play-fullness promises less stress and anxiety with a stronger sense of belonging, deeper intimacy, friendships that flourish, and a spirit that is nurtured in relationship with God and all of God's creation.

The Wish, the Fear, and Other Questions

In life, the same things we wish for are often the very things we fear. We long for a play-full life, yet we consciously or unconsciously fear how it will affect the life we know. We long for intimacy with self and others, yet we fear losing ourselves in the process or we fear our inability to sustain intimacy. As you reach the end of this book, you might still ask: *How do I achieve a play-full life?* Or, *How will I know that I am being play-full?* Business consultant Peter Block argues that the answer to such "How?" questions is always a simple "Yes!" Say Yes! to the many small ways this book encourages you to seek peace and a sense of justice within yourself and between you and others and God. Say Yes! to a life shown to us by Christ Jesus, a life that invites us into a personal relationship with him and that calls us to love ourselves and others and practice hospitality. Say Yes! to a life that is not intrinsically motivated, but that originates from a Higher source, from the God we know as Earth Maker, Pain Bearer, and Life Giver. Motivated by this God, play-fullness is best not imagined, but lived. Say Yes! to a life that you may not "achieve" in the way the enemies of play-fullness would envision perfection, for your play-fullness will continue through and beyond your death as you are reunited with your Creator and Savior. That we can practice play-fullness yet not achieve perfection in being play-full is one more tension we can hold in our ever-expanding inner space. If you hold this tension, the unachievable nature of play-fullness will not bring criticism or the need for control, but rather it will infuse you with a sense of being real and the invitation to experience boundlessness.

Embracing play-fullness goes beyond the many possible activities described in these pages. Begin with something simple, such as consuming less, refraining from criticizing people, cooking your own meals, or holding the many tensions in your reality. Or begin by taking a different way home, playing with the acronym PLAY-FULL, which stands for . . . or by praying an honest prayer. There is such potential in being play-full that play, and not necessity, has been described as the mother of invention. Play is the mother of invention since we are created into the image of the God of invention.

In life, an important task is figuring out which questions should be asked and which ones need not be entertained. The question is never: *Am I play-full?* but always, *How play-full am I?* There's no need to ask: *Why can't I be more play-full?* but ask: *How can I increase my play-fullness just a bit?* Having been created in the image of God that portrays Realness, Boundlessness, Slowness, Creativity, Hospitality, and Transcendence, you had kernels of play-fullness before you picked up this book.

Maybe you had to think awhile in order to locate yourself on this imaginary scale, but I imagine you found an answer to this last question of naming something you can do to increase your play-fullness. That's how God made us. We almost always know what we can do to better our lives, even though at times we find it difficult to implement what we know will serve us well. If you do feel stuck in being play-full, engage any of the play-full practices described here, or identify which of the enemies of play-fullness are most active in your life and address them intentionally. Spend time with someone who is play-full, possibly a child, and it's likely that you will become unstuck. Ask God to restore you to your created being and show you ways to be more play-full.

---

10 = you are as play-full as you can be

1 = you are not play-full at all

Rank yourself:

- Where would you have ranked yourself before you read this book?
- Where do you rank yourself at this moment?
- What can you do to move up one notch on this scale?

Play-fullness, as you've discovered, can inform your life even in moments of struggle and pain. When you practice play-fullness, remind yourself that the West sees practice as acquiring a skill, while the East sees practice as creating a person. Maybe we can learn something from our sisters and brothers in the East. Regardless, be intentional as you form an authentic self and soul and the many relationships you keep as someone deeply rooted in life and God.

Trusting Life and Thinking outside the Box

One of the functions of childhood play is to instill a sense of trust within the child and to help the child find creative ways to engage an ever-expanding reality. So too does play-fullness instill a sense of trust in us as we recognize the goodness and the gift of life, community, and the grace of God. Through play-fullness we experience the excitement of an unfolding reality. The enemies of play-fullness do not determine this reality as they want us to believe, but God reigns. Like Elisha's servant who saw chariots of fire all around him and found his fears were removed, so too we recognize God's reign in this world. The enemies of play-fullness, serving their lord of destruction, become disempowered as peace sets in and as justice is sought, whether justice for the earth by consuming less or justice for persons and groups marginalized by extending hospitality to them.

How would you describe the meaning
you have discovered in being play-full?

A play-full life is thus a hopeful and spiritual life, which, in our materialistic and paranoid world, is thinking outside the box. Such a life sees reality with new eyes, eyes that allow for something good coming toward us. Play-fullness anticipates; it is being on an adventure. What is coming might be an internal shift you make, it might come in the form of another person or persons, or it might be about discovering God anew. Without doubt, you will experience God's peace — God's *shalom* — as you experience awe, wonder, rapture, and enthusiasm, a peace that may even transcend all understanding. As a play-full person, you not only seek peace and justice; you also participate in God's *shalom* — that special experience your inner space knows well, an experience that's repeated between you and others, and that you witness in the world. You'll find yourself in a "thin" place where God is near.

When you trust life and God with play-fullness, the promise of a life and relationships rejuvenated and revitalized is yours. As play-fullness enriches your body, mind, spirit, and all your relation-ships, you'll again discover that wholeness and health is defined not by the *absence* of dis-ease or disease but by the *presence* of meaning. The meaning (the fruit) of play-fullness is being real and boundless, practicing slowness, being creative and hospitable, and experiencing transcendence and meeting the Transcendent.

Trust, health, and wholeness take us back to being intentional and committed, to being present to yourself, others, and to God in a world that is trying its best to keep you distracted and going at full speed. The process and practice of living creatively is transformative and a gift you receive *within* yourself, *between* you and the world, and (*without*) from God. God has given you permission to be.

Work, Play, or a Feast?

As I wrote A *Play-full Life,* a diverse group of readers gave me feedback on the chapter drafts as they appeared. They often asked about what I experience as I read, contemplate, and write: Is writing a book on being play-full work or play? Does your custom of writing during the early morning hours before your family awakens reflect the nature of the project?

For me, a book project works best if I can say that the book wrote me even as I wrote the book. This is very true for A *Play-full Life.* I experienced all the play-full practices in increasing fashion as the book took form. Slowness was the first practice I met as I quickly discovered I could not write this book in the academic style I know so well, the only style my life of education has taught me. I did many revisions, and that slowed the project down considerably. Twice I asked the publisher for a manuscript submission extension, while working all along. Realness set in as I recognized I am a writer who does not know how to write. Boundlessness was present as my increased play-fullness flowed into my most intimate relationships. I became more creative in that I needed to let go of preconceived ideas and allow the project to take new form. The two plus hours I spent every morning became a hospitable time. So too was working over my lunch hours. I felt welcomed into a space that I always left with new energy, my mind writing additional paragraphs and my spirit giving me new ideas to be typed out the next morning. Some mornings I felt stuck and didn't know how to proceed. So I would just type, often doing word-play or reflecting on stories from Scripture that touch me deeply, fully aware that everything I wrote I might delete the very next morning. Yet always these "unproductive" mornings showed me new pathways to explore as if bringing the project back on track. Many mornings I discovered something new about God and myself, and often this was an invitation to slow down with God and enter into deeper intimacy with God and others.

Often I would wake before the usual 4:50 a.m. summons from the alarm clock, anticipating a time of drinking Rooibos tea, being greeted by Milo (the cat) who flops on her back for a belly rub, and listening as the birds greeted the morning. Spending the next two hours with my thoughts about play-fullness was sacred time. I will miss it when I no longer follow this rhythm even though I will enjoy the extra sleep that awaits me. Yes, writing this book was sometimes work, but most often it was a play-full time that energized me and brought me back to the dining room table morning after morning. Ultimately, the book wrote me. I am becoming play-full.

Jesus offers you life to the full. Water turns into wine. People are fed and healed. Life under this promise of God is being invited to a banquet. The word is out on the street that a feast has been prepared and that the original guests have declined the invitation. Now there's an open invitation to all people to come and eat. You too are invited to this feast. Every day is a good day to be play-full. Begin today!

Resources

Andrews, Geoff. *The Slow Food Story*. Ithaca, N.Y.: McGill-Queens University Press, 2008.

Aron, Cindy Sondik. *Working at Play: A History of Vacations in the United States*. New York: Oxford University Press, 1999.

Berryman, Jerome. *Teaching Godly Play: The Sunday Morning Handbook*. Minneapolis: Augsburg Fortress Press, 1995.

Block, Peter. *The Answer to How Is Yes: Acting on What Matters*. San Francisco: Berrett-Koehler Publishers, 2002.

Borg, Marcus J. *Jesus, a New Vision: Spirit, Culture, and the Life of Discipleship*. San Francisco: Harper & Row, 1987.

Brannen, Barbara. *The Gift of Play: Why Adult Women Stop Playing and How to Start Again*. New York: Writers Club Press, 2002.

Brown, Stuart, and Christopher Vaughan. *Play: How It Shapes the Brain, Opens the Imagination, and Invigorates the Soul*. New York: Avery, 2009.

Buber, Martin, and Walter A. Kaufmann. *I and Thou*. New York: Scribner, 1970.

Caillois, Roger, and Meyer Barash. *Man, Play, and Games*. Urbana: University of Illinois Press, 2001.

Capps, Donald. *Agents of Hope: A Pastoral Psychology*. Minneapolis: Fortress Press, 1995.

Carse, James P. *Finite and Infinite Games: A Vision of Life as Play and Possibility*. New York: Free Press, 1986.

Cohen, David. *The Development of Play*. 3rd ed. London and New York: Routledge, 2006.

Cohen, Lawrence J. *Playful Parenting: A Bold New Way to Nurture Close Connections, Solve Behavior Problems, and Encourage Children's Confidence*. 1st ed. New York: Ballantine Books, 2001.

Cross, Gary S., and John K. Walton. *The Playful Crowd: Pleasure Places in the Twentieth Century*. New York: Columbia University Press, 2005.

Duncan, David James. *God Laughs and Plays: Churchless Sermons in Response to the Preachments of the Fundamentalist Right*. Great Barrington, Mass.: Triad Institute, 2006.

Duncan, Margaret Carlisle, Garry Chick, and Alan Aycock, eds. *Play and Culture Studies*. Greenwich, Conn.: Ablex Pub. Co., 1998.

Elkind, David. *The Power of Play: How Spontaneous, Imaginative Activities Lead to Happier, Healthier Children*. Cambridge: Da Capo Press, 2007.

Erikson, Erik H. *Toys and Reasons: Stages in the Ritualization of Experience*. 1st ed. New York: Norton, 1977.

Forencich, Frank. *Exuberant Animal: Riffs on Human Health, Play and Joyful Movement*. Seattle, Wash.: GoAnimal, 2006.

Gini, A. *Importance of Being Lazy: In Praise of Play, Leisure, and Vacations*. New York: London: Routledge, 2003.

Goldman, Dodi. *In Search of the Real: The Origins and Originality of D. W. Winnicott*. Northvale, N.J.: Jason Aronson Press, 1993.

Grant, Brian W. *A Theology for Pastoral Psychotherapy: God's Play in Sacred Spaces*. New York: Haworth Pastoral Press, 2001.

Gronick, Simon A. *The Work and Play of Winnicott*. Northvale, N.J.: Jason Aronson, 1990.

Hamman, Jaco J. *When Steeples Cry: Leading Congregations through Loss and Change*. Cleveland: Pilgrim Press, 2005.

———. *Becoming a Pastor: Forming Self and Soul for Ministry*. Cleveland: Pilgrim Press, 2007.

Honoré, Carl. *In Praise of Slowness: How a Worldwide Movement Is Challenging the Cult of Speed*. 1st ed. San Francisco: HarperSanFrancisco, 2004.

Huizinga, Johan. *Homo Ludens: A Study of the Play-Element in Culture*. Boston: Beacon Press, 1955.

Koppel, Michael S. *Open-Hearted Ministry: Play as Key to Pastoral Leadership*. Minneapolis: Fortress Press, 2008.

Landreth, Garry L. *Play Therapy: The Art of the Relationship*. 2nd ed. New York: Brunner-Routledge, 2002.

Martyn, Dorothy W. *Beyond Deserving: Children, Parents, and Responsibility Revisited*. Grand Rapids, Mich.: Eerdmans, 2007.

McCarthy, Barry W., and Emily J. McCarthy. *Rekindling Desire: A Step-by-Step Program to Help Low-Sex and No-Sex Marriages*. New York: Brunner-Routledge, 2003.

Meares, Russell. *The Metaphor of Play: Origin and Breakdown of Personal Being*. 3rd ed. London and New York: Routledge, 2005.

Miller, David LeRoy. *Gods and Games: Toward a Theology of Play*. New York: Harper & Row Publishers, 1973.

Miller-McLemore, Bonnie J. *In the Midst of Chaos: Caring for Children as Spiritual Practice*. San Francisco: Jossey-Bass, 2006.

Moltmann, Jürgen, Robert E. Neale, Sam Keen, and David LeRoy Miller. *Theology of Play*. New York: Harper & Row, 1972.

Nachmanovitch, Stephen. *Free Play: Improvisation in Life and Art*. 1st ed. Los Angeles: J. P. Tarcher, 1990.

Neale, Robert E. *In Praise of Play: Toward a Psychology of Religion.* New York: Harper & Row, 1969.

Neville, Graham. *Free Time: Towards a Theology of Leisure.* Birmingham, U.K.: University of Birmingham, 2004.

Paley, Vivian Gussin. *You Can't Say You Can't Play.* Cambridge, Mass.: Harvard University Press, 1992.

Peterson, Eugene H. *Christ Plays in Ten Thousand Places: A Conversation in Spiritual Theology.* Grand Rapids, Mich.: Eerdmans, 2005.

Petrini, Carlo. *Slow Food: The Case for Taste.* New York: Columbia University Press, 2003.

Petrini, Carlo, and Gigi Padovani. *Slow Food Revolution: A New Culture for Eating and Living.* New York: Rizzoli, 2006.

Phillips, Adam. *Going Sane: Maps of Happiness.* New York: Fourth Estate, 2005.

Phillips, Adam, and Barbara Taylor. *On Kindness.* New York: Farrar, Straus and Giroux, 2009.

Pruyser, Paul W. *The Play of the Imagination: Towards a Psychoanalysis of Culture.* New York: International Universities Press, 1983.

Rahner, Hugo. *Man at Play.* New York: Herder & Herder, 1967.

Schweitzer, Carol L. Schnabl. *The Stranger's Voice: Julia Kristeva's Relevance for a Pastoral Theology for Women Struggling with Depression.* Practical Theology. New York: Peter Lang, 2010.

Sutton-Smith, Brian. *The Ambiguity of Play.* Cambridge, Mass.: Harvard University Press, 1997.

Taylor, Barbara Brown. *An Altar in the World: A Geography of Faith.* 1st ed. New York: HarperOne, 2009.

Terr, Lenore. *Beyond Love and Work: Why Adults Need to Play.* New York: Scribner, 1999.

Wilson, Eric. *Against Happiness: In Praise of Melancholy.* New York: Farrar, Straus and Giroux, 2009.

Winnicott, Donald W. *Playing and Reality.* London: Tavistock, 1993.

Websites

Community Supported Agriculture: *www.localharvest.org*
MotherTongues: *www.mothertongues.com*
National Institute for Play: *www.nifplay.org*
Slow Living: *www.slowmovement.com; www.slowplanet.com*
The Story of Stuff: *www.storyofstuff.com*